EARTH RIGHT

Publisher's Statement

As part of our commitment to upholding the principles in this important book, Prima has printed this book on Cross Pointe Troy recycled paper. In addition, we are committed to following the principles outlined in *EarthRight*, including recycling metals, glass, plastics, and wherever possible, paper.

How to Order:

Quantity discounts are available from the publisher, Prima Publishing & Communications, P.O. Box 1260PH, Rocklin, CA 95677; telephone (916) 624-5718. On your letterhead include information concerning the intended use of the books and the number of books you wish to purchase.

U.S. Bookstores and Libraries: Please submit all orders to St. Martin's Press, 175 Fifth Avenue, New York, NY 10010; telephone (212) 674-5151.

EARTH RIGHT

H. Patricia Hynes

Department of Urban Studies
M.I.T.

This book is printed on recycled paper.

Prima Publishing & Communications
P.O. Box 1260PH
Rocklin, CA 95677
(916) 624-5718

Typography by Howarth & Smith Limited
Copyediting by Victoria Nelson
Production by Rosaleen Bertolino, Bookman Productions
Jacket design by The Dunlavey Studio
Illustrations by George Ulrich

Prima Publishing & Communications

Library of Congress Cataloging-in-Publication Data

Hynes, H. Patricia.
    EarthRight: what you can do in your home, workplace, and community to save our environment / H. Patricia Hynes.
        p. cm.
    Includes bibliographical references.
    ISBN 1-55958-028-3. — ISBN 1-55958-027-5 (pbk.)
    1. Environmental protection—Citizen participation. I. Title.
TD170.2.H96   1990
363.7'0757—dc20   89-48542
                                                                                                          CIP

90 91 92 93 RRD 10 9 8 7 6 5 4 3 2 1

Printed in the United States of America

To my mother, Helen G.,
and my father, Thomas V.,
for moments that stay

Preface

Almost every Sunday in the summers of my childhood, my parents would take their nine children to a farm on the Chesapeake Canal. "The farm" was the country vacation home of my uncle and aunt and six cousins. Our days there were full of outdoor play. We swam in the canal. We roamed the old barn and musty sheds searching for signs of their former farm life. We picked strawberries, blackberries, two kinds of raspberries, and wild blueberries. We walked through long stretches of woods—always alert for snakes—to visit our nearest neighbors, Ukrainian farmers, whose farm was a real one, with manure smells and chicken droppings all over the place.

Memories of the farm swarmed about me as I wrote *EarthRight*: the dusk calls of whippoorwill and bobwhite; standing in beachgrass at sunset with only the low, lapping sound of an incoming tide interrupting the stillness; a mammoth beech tree with smooth, gray bark like elephant skin—a tree that was nearly as wide as I was tall and whose broad reach of branches shaded the cars parked beneath it; fields of wild grass and black-eyed susans that drifted down to clayey cliffs overhanging the canal; and in every direction beyond the fields, forests, as far as the eye could see. I thank Aunt Martha and Uncle John for this nearness to nature that city life—as it is designed—is devoid of.

EarthRight began with a phone call and conversation. Charlotte Raymond, my agent, called me one afternoon in late September 1988 and proposed the idea of *EarthRight*. I am grateful to her for the inspiration and for her deep interest in every detail of this book. After the call, the next two hours were spent with Jan Raymond and Eileen Barrett, brainstorming on the issues I should select for *EarthRight*. The book took shape that evening, and the course that I set has never shifted.

The beginning was auspicious; so also, the finishing. Those engaged in its production—publisher Ben Dominitz, editor Patti Breitman, production editor Rosaleen Bertolino, and illustrator George Ulrich—have worked skillfully and energetically for *EarthRight*.

While writing this book, I received an enormous amount of resource material and assistance from friends, associates, and even strangers who took special interest in *EarthRight*. Here I mention only those whose contribution was especially beneficial: Robin Ellis, Marge Hynes, Karen Jones, Steve Bastide, Elana Marton, Elizabeth Lambert, Lewis Bernard, Alice Hanley Raymond, Earl Raymond, and Amy Hines. The studies and activist work of many institutions were invaluable; among them are the Massachusetts Audubon Society, the Environmental Defense Fund, the Natural Resources Defense Council, the Rainforest Action Network, Worldwatch Institute, and the Institute for Local Self-Reliance. The Shawmut Bank of Hampshire County generously provided financial support for *EarthRight*.

Almost daily there is news of worsening environmental conditions. This unhappy reality can make informational books on the environment out of date before they are published. *EarthRight*, however, is not only an informational book; it is a book about informed action. The actions I recommend here will always be necessary if we truly want to *make amends* to our planet and to live on Earth in ways that are *just, appropriate, most favorable,* and *genuine* (all meanings of the word *right*).

Contents

Introduction

The Earth does not belong to [us], [we] belong to the Earth.
Chief Seattle to President Franklin Pierce

I began *EarthRight* in the summer of 1988 because wherever I looked the environment was under siege. "The Earth fighting back" is how one journalist described the acute events of 1988. Medical waste floated onto public beaches in North Jersey, Long Island, Connecticut, Massachusetts, and as far north as Maine. That same summer, a drought persisted in the Midwest agriculture belt with a severity not seen since the Dust Bowl phenomenon of the 1930s. The drought coincided with a record heat wave throughout much of the country, which climatologists suspect is part of a trend in global warming. Recently we were told by NASA that the ozone layer over Antarctica is being depleted at a faster rate than any experts had forecast. This news caused the Environmental Protection Agency (EPA) to admit that the new international treaty to limit ozone-depleting chemicals, the 1987 Montreal Protocol, is already outdated. Hardly a day has passed since I began writing *EarthRight* when the daily newspapers I read have failed to carry stories of the crisis in solid waste, with landfills rapidly filling up and their alternative—municipal incinerators—generating dioxins. In April 1989, a single-hulled ship spilled millions of gallons of oil into Arctic waters.

Disruption of climate and the atmosphere along with contamination of the seas have shaken people for whom a clean environment had previously been an issue second to their pocketbooks, education, property values, drugs, and AIDS. Issues of keeping harbors clean and preserving wilderness have moved from second-level to first-level political campaign concerns alongside national security and national debt.

Is this acceleration of pollution the Earth striking back? As chief of Environmental Management at the Massachusetts Port Authority and section chief in the EPA's Hazardous Waste Division, I had to solve pollution problems as diverse as abandoned hazardous waste dumps, leaking underground storage tanks, asbestos removal, and lead paint on bridges. But the environmental problems of 1988 were of a magnitude and complexity we had not previously seen. Record smog levels over remote Mt. Desert Island and plastics killing sea mammals are not signals that the Earth is fighting back. On the contrary, they are dramatic evidence that environmental protection is not working as well as we thought and cannot be left to government agencies and small numbers of activists. This breakdown of the vast, seemingly untouchable systems of climate, atmosphere, and ocean makes us feel powerless before the enormous consequences of their pollution, and often hopeless about solutions. Faced with our seeming powerlessness, I contend that it is we who can *and must* fight back.

What is vast—like the stratospheric ozone layer—reaches into our lives and touches them individually. Should we spend as much time in the sun or encourage children to do so, if skin cancer rates will increase dramatically with a depleted ozone layer? What we do in the privacy of our lives ripples out and affects the vast. Cars are a major single source of air pollution and global warming. Do we carpool and use public transportation whenever possible? What we do personally and locally, such as the amount and kind of trash we generate, has extensive consequence for the atmosphere and aquifers. Styrofoam cups and packaging are linked with depletion of the ozone layer. Pesticides and waste oil thrown into garbage, which is then buried in the town landfill, can contaminate the town's drinking water wells.

Many of us fight contradictory feelings in the face of the lengthening chain of environmental disasters: powerlessness and hopelessness before their magnitude, and a desire *to do something* to make them less inevitable. *EarthRight* is written at this interface of global pollution and personal action. It is a guide to taking action, intended to empower you with practical knowledge so that you will know how to make a difference. It is not meant to be a substitute for the negligence of government and industry. It is meant to show, rather, that we do not have to stand by idly and watch their negligence, nor leave the protection of the environment solely in their hands.

So often, when I have spoken at environmental conferences and to community groups organized to fight against hazardous waste sites in their neighborhoods, I have witnessed how environmental issues catalyze people. The environment arouses elemental feelings about the future of life on the planet. Environmental pollution of the scope we are witnessing makes people question whether the so-called "American way of life" is not purchased at the expense of something more precious: coexistence with nature. I am convinced that many people want to take personal action to stem the tide of global pollution, that they would like to live well but not at the expense of the atmosphere, climate, oceans, and other creatures with whom we share this Earth. I am also convinced that, if connections between their choices and pollution are clear, many people are willing to waste less, conserve more, and make decisions with the environment in mind.

This willingness to "live as if the Earth mattered" has been measured and confirmed recently by various surveys. *Time*, for example, published a questionnaire in its January 2, 1989 issue in which the Endangered Earth was chosen as Planet of the Year in lieu of the usual Man or rare Woman of the Year. Readers were asked two questions: Are you willing to pay 50¢ per gallon more in gasoline taxes to spur fuel conservation? Would you separate your garbage in order to facilitate recycling? As of late June 1989, nearly 12,000 replied. Seventy-seven percent supported the gas tax proposal; ninety-five percent were willing to separate their garbage. *What are you willing to do?*

In late spring 1989, a syndicated columnist lamented that we need another hot, dry summer to forge the political will for tough environmental measures. Just before his article appeared, the *Exxon Valdez* hit the well-known and well-charted Bligh Reef, ran aground off the coast of southern Alaska, and spilled 10.9 million gallons of crude oil into pristine Prince William Sound. Since then, three simultaneous spills dumped oil into Narragansett Bay, the Delaware River, and the Gulf of Mexico off the coast of Texas. I believe the environmental disasters of 1988 and 1989—each year seems to bring new and more cataclysmic ones—are sufficiently etched into our consciousness that we do not need another graphic proof of global emergency to catalyze the will for change. As I watched people sponge off oil-soaked Alaskan sea birds and otters in limited but infinitely caring gestures, I was reminded of the words of the Suquamish Indian Chief Seattle to President Franklin Pierce. "If all the beasts were gone . . . [we] would die of a great loneliness."

I wrote *EarthRight* to provide lucid, accessible, and practical ideas about reversing environmental destruction for people in search of them. *EarthRight* devotes one part each to five major problems: pesticides, solid waste and plastics, contaminated drinking water, depletion of the ozone layer, and global warming. These five areas do not exhaust the pollution issues, but they are the ones that preoccupy the press and that are uppermost in people's minds. The depletion of the ozone layer and global warming are the most unpredictable and possibly catastrophic effects of human activities on the planet: reason enough to come to grips with them here. Contaminated drinking water and pesticides in the garden and food supply are older problems, closer to home but very persistent, that environmental agencies have not solved. It is time to move beyond just protecting ourselves from pollution with individual solutions like buying bottled water and organic produce; we must go to the source of the problem and start there. Thus this guide features a water protection plan for municipal drinking water supplies as one starting point. The plan features the commonsensical idea of zoning industry with hazardous chemical activity and the water supply in different sectors of a city.

Each section in *EarthRight* has a similar format: (1) a comprehensive, nontechnical explanation of the causes of the pollution problem and its known and possible effects on people's health and ecosystems; (2) a series of actions people can take in their own lives, communities, and workplaces that can help prevent or lessen the problem; and (3) a resource section that provides the names of projects, institutes, agencies, organizations, and publications for further information and involvement.

Illustrations have been included to demystify technical concepts that might otherwise be inaccessible to the general public. For example, Part 3 uses illustrations with text to trace a city's drinking water from its source in an aquifer or river through the water storage and treatment plant to the consumer's home. En route many possible sources of pollution, such as gas stations, herbicide spraying under utilities' rights-of-way, road salt, and septic systems are included to show the connections between a town's chemical use and the contamination of its drinking water. The same principles apply to the connections between private drinking water wells, septic systems, and lawn care chemicals; only the scale is different. You will learn how to develop maps of your own drinking water source and to inventory the possible sources of pollution in their water supply. You will also learn how to have your tap water analyzed, what chemicals to look for, whether or not a laboratory is certified for the analysis, how to eliminate the contaminants, and how to avoid them in the first place.

The stories of ordinary people amplify the information on "what you can do"—people like June Larson, who because of her daughter's illness initiated the "right-to-know" movement for posting warnings on property when pesticides are used; and Sarah Blair and Maria Valenti, two women who started a bimonthly newsletter of practical suggestions for trading in toxic hazards for safe alternatives. Also featured are those cities and states that have adopted creative environmental ordinances: The states of Vermont and Hawaii have limited the emissions of chlorofluorocarbons; the city of Seattle has set a goal of recycling up to sixty percent of its solid waste. The reader will learn of an industry's "buy recycled" policy and the "styrofoam-free" policy instituted by a public agency. Their example serves as beacons to enlighten us, and models to prod and encourage us to "go and do likewise."

Most people live local lives. Many get bewildered and feel increasingly bleak before things as large as global problems. Who really believes that beached whales, extended heat waves, and pollution of the sea symbolize the Earth striking back? On the contrary, these realities make us suspect that the earth is falling apart and wish that *we* could fight back to save our global home. People recognize that the Earth is more polluted than it was ten years ago because pollution is seeping into their lives in ways they have never seen before. Knowledge gives reason to act; and action, in the face of something inevitable and frightening, is empowering. Action gives hope; hope supports action. These reinforcing cycles are offered here as an alternative to the downward spiral of pollution and the depressing sense of the inevitable that follows in its wake.

Popular explanations of the garbage crisis abound; so do government studies on contaminated drinking water and pesticides in the food supply. Scholarly science journals feature numerous articles on global warming and the fate of the ozone layer. Activist groups like the San Francisco-based Rainforest Action Network have prepared fact sheets to simplify the connections between global warming and fast-food hamburgers made from cattle that graze on vegetation in destroyed rainforests. Some of this information is accessible to the general public. A lot is not: Because it is written too technically; because it is scattered in disparate contexts and not yet brought together in one practical guide; and because the majority of people are not yet affiliated with environmental organizations, which distribute their studies and reports to their members. This guide draws from all of these sources and also from interviews with research scientists to provide basic, nontechnical, yet thorough explanations of environmental pollution. It does not presume insider knowledge or experience, though it does presume a willingness to tackle tough ideas. The recommendations in each chapter for taking action use and build on what individuals and groups are achieving in neighborhoods, offices, and companies across the United States. My own experience in preparing a water supply protection by-law for the town of Montague, Massachusetts serves as a firsthand example of the difference one person can make.

An early defense of the space program was the astronauts' unitive pictures of Earth as a fragile blue and green globe spinning in space. This image, supporters forecast, would forever change the limited, regional way we see ourselves. We would know from that point forward that in some fundamental and irreversible way we were citizens of the planet. But it took a nuclear accident in Chernobyl—more than these mystical, outer-space photos of Earth—and the belts of radiation it sent to encircle the Northern Hemisphere to shock humankind into seeing how small and irreversibly interconnected our world really is.

Pollution knows no boundaries. More people understood the consequences of this fact after the summer of 1988 and the largest oil spill in U.S. history in spring 1989. More people are prepared to think globally because of the perversity of pollution. Now is the time to "act locally." *EarthRight* shows how.

EARTH
RIGHT

PART ONE

Pesticides: Poisons in a Progressive Package

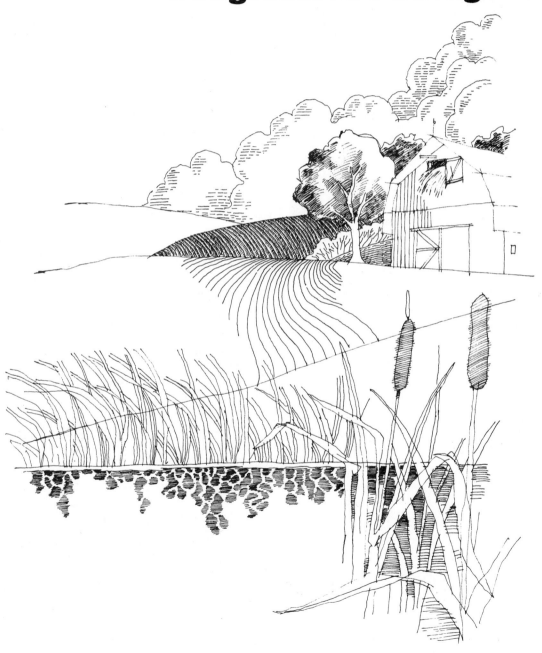

The earth's vegetation is part of a web of life in which there are intimate and essential relations between plants and the earth, between plants and other plants, between plants and animals. Sometimes we have no choice but to disturb these relationships, but we should do so thoughtfully, with full awareness that what we do may have consequences remote in time and place.

Rachel Carson, *Silent Spring* (1962)

The overwhelming tragedy of planet Earth is man's contempt for nature.

Robert van den Bosch, *The Pesticide Conspiracy* (1978)

Remember the slogan, "Better Living Through Chemistry"? This motto sold nylon, teflon, and pesticides all in the same breath. Sometime mid-century the new synthetic chemical pesticides—DDT, aldrin, dieldrin, chlordane, and other strange-sounding but instant household names—became necessary for better homes, better gardens and "better living."

In 1962, Rachel Carson put the pesticide industry and pesticide-based agriculture on trial with the publication of *Silent Spring*. Pesticides were sprayed lavishly across the United States in the late 1940s and 1950s, and they were promoted as the panacea for world famine and plague. Carson cut through the promotional veil to expose the hazards of modern pesticide use to animal and human life. She warned that pesticides are acutely toxic chemicals, which should be used cautiously and as a last, not first, resort.

As *Silent Spring* was being published, however, the Monsanto Company, a major manufacturer of chemical pesticides, rushed the galley sheets of "The Desolate Year" through corporate chain of command. This pamphlet portrays a world without pesticides. Bugs march across the United States like Sherman's army to the sea, destroying everything in their path. Farmers plant and cultivate, but they harvest garbage. Food processors find produce so insect-ridden they can hardly handle it, and the Food and Drug Administration can't approve it. Food grows scarce; prices spiral upwards, and the world belongs to the insects. Under siege but emasculated without chemical weapons, the country is helpless to fight its foes, the insect hordes.

This parody of *Silent Spring* was in keeping with a specific world view. The explosive production, promotion, and use of chemical pesticides since 1945 was based on the metaphor of war, with insects as enemies, chemicals as weapons, farmers as combatants, and pesticide manufacturers as military strategists. This was fitting because many of the new pesticides were originally developed for chemical warfare. When World War II ended, markets were needed for a peacetime use of the chemicals.

The central ideas of *Silent Spring* are as important today as in 1962, for two reasons. Although *Silent Spring* was a thorough exposé of the hazards of pesticide residues in food supply and the food chain and set in motion reform of pesticide regulation, four to five times the quantity of pesticides are used today as were used in 1962. The second reason is the one for which *Silent Spring* was written: In nature, nothing exists alone. A pesticide sprayed on a potato field will be absorbed into the plant roots and tissue, where it acts as a systemic poison to insects. Some residue washes through the soil into groundwater and is drawn to a drinking water well where it is pumped to the kitchen tap. Other residue is eroded with soil into a nearby stream where it is ingested by insect larvae, which are eaten by a fish. The fish is eaten by another fish, a bird, a wetland animal, or a human being.

DDT was banned from extensive use in the United States in 1972. Yet traces of DDT are still found in mammals' milk, sperm, and body fat; in the sediments of lakes, rivers, and harbors; and in fish. Since 1972, DDT and other pesticides prohibited from use in the United States because of their toxicity and persistence in the food chain have still been manufactured for use in developing countries. They are then imported back to this country in fruits and vegetables in part of what is called a "circle of poison."

And, lest we focus only on the half of the circle that recirculates the poisons to us in imported food, listen to the stories I heard at a recent international environmental conference, the Congress on the

Fate and Hope of the Earth, held in Managua, Nicaragua, in June 1989. A labor organizer of agricultural workers described pesticide spray drifting into farm workers' soup bowls in Zimbabwe coffee plantations as they ate their lunch under shade trees on the edge of the agricultural field. Many feed their babies on their lunch break; others carry them, sleeping, on their backs. A Central American health worker described how one pesticide was routinely used for fishing: Once the pesticide was dumped into a pond, dead fish quickly floated to the top. Both speakers told us that safety instructions, even when they are in the right language, are useless to farm workers and peasants who don't read.

Pesticides are an "old" environmental problem that needs fresh action.

Chapter 1

A Primer on Pesticides

Pesticide is a general word for poisons, poisons that control or kill insects, fungi, weeds, and rodents. Some pesticides prolong the storage life of produce; others are used to keep produce free of blemishes. Some experts think that the most widely used pesticides on citrus fruit control a pest that causes only cosmetic damage.

Take Alar, a trade name for the chemical daminozide, as an example of nonessential uses of a dangerous pesticide. Alar is a plant growth regulator registered in 1963 and used, until recently, on almost half of the U.S. apple crop. Treated with daminozide, apples redden more deeply and uniformly, ripen more slowly, and are less likely to drop from trees, making harvesting easier. This chemical, which causes five types of cancer in toxicity tests, breaks down into a potent carcinogen when apples are processed into products like applesauce and apple juice. Like hundreds of pesticides, Alar is an older pesticide that has not come under the more recent, stricter review process for registering pesticides. In 1985, the Environmental Protection Agency proposed to cancel the uses of daminozide on food, but then it softened this position and allowed the manufacturer, the Uniroyal Chemical Company, to conduct further tests on the chemical. These tests found residues of the pesticide and its breakdown products in the majority of test samples of apple products, peanuts, and peanut butter. The chemical continued to be used.

This information was highlighted in February 1989, when the Natural Resources Defense Council released a major study on the health effects, especially for children, of agricultural pesticides. At the same time, a campaign entitled *Mothers and Others for Pesticide*

5

Limits was launched. Chaired by the actress Meryl Streep, the campaign galvanized attention on a carcinogenic pesticide—Alar—used for cosmetic purposes on apples, a mainstay of children's diets. Almost immediately there was an explosion of demand for Alar-free apples, apple juice and applesauce, and organic produce in general. Several supermarket chains announced they would stop selling apples treated with Alar; some food manufacturers stopped using Alar-treated apples in their apple products.

The next month, the *New York Times* carried an article entitled, "A Harvest of Organic Produce in the Wake of Pesticide Fears." In April, the *Boston Globe* featured two New England producers of organic baby food. In May, the *Wall Street Journal* carried an article, "A Movement to Farm Without Chemicals Makes Surprising Gains." The same month, the *New York Times* reported on some of the country's largest farms in California that began experimenting with growing fruits and vegetables without synthetic chemicals in a story, "Big Farm Companies Try Hand at Organic Methods." Growers were planting vetch, a legume, to provide nitrogen instead of fertilizers. Weeds would be removed with hoes and mechanical cultivators instead of with herbicides. Parasitic insects and predators would be introduced to help keep down insect pests. One company built a prototype vacuum cleaner mounted on board a grape harvesting machine to suck insects off the vines. By fall 1989, the number of organic farms in California had doubled within a year to about 1,500. In addition, thousands of other California farms used pesticides only as a last resort.

Fresh action against an old problem was dramatic and immediate. In May 1989 the International Apple Institute, an industry trade group, announced that U.S. growers, who had already lost $50 million from a sharp drop in sales, would suspend Alar on apples by fall 1989. The same month the Waxman-Kennedy Food Safety Amendments of 1989 were introduced into Congress by a bill that closes many of the loopholes in current pesticide-in-food regulation. In June, Uniroyal halted domestic sales of Alar.

Throughout the spring, articles with titles like "Fears of Pesticides Threaten American Way of Farming" were popping up like weeds, articles that turned the benefits of food supply without pesticides into a liability for those who manufacture and use the pesticides. The tide against lacing a food supply with toxic substances is coming in, however, and a spring tide it is.

The production of synthetic pesticides in the United States soared after World War II, increasing more than fivefold between 1947 and 1960 to about 650 million pounds. Today more than 2.5 billion pounds of pesticides are now used each year—on agricultural crops, in forests, on ponds and lakes, on golf courses, in city parks, and in homes. Farmers and the food supply industry apply the largest amounts of pesticides to kill weeds, fumigate soil, kill insect pests and control plant diseases, and for cosmetic purposes—nearly 1 billion pounds. As a result of such intensive use, insect resistance to pesticides has grown to the point that ever-increasing amounts of pesticides need to be used. Groundwater contamination in agricultural areas is common. Farm workers in California, where pesticides are used more intensively than anywhere in the world, have the highest rate of occupational illness. And pesticide residues contaminate the food supply.

INSECT RESISTANCE

With the intensive application of pesticides since World War II, the number of insect species resistant to chemicals began a meteoric rise. Before 1945, about a dozen species were known to have developed resistance to pre-DDT insecticides, whereas by 1960 as many as 137 species were known to be resistant to the new pesticides. The government and industry response to resistance was to spray more intensively and more frequently, creating more resistant species and thus aggravating the problem they were alleged to solve. There are now more than 440 insect species resistant to insecticides. Over twenty species are immune to all pesticides in use.

Insects survive insecticides with the same plasticity that enabled them to survive drastic changes in climate and habitat over the millennia. Some carry the genetic capability to detoxify the poison in the spray; others are physically protected by an outer covering that prevents the penetration of the toxic material; still others are simply missed by the spray or avoid it. With multiple sprayings, those insects that survive because of a natural resistance come to dominate the population and reproduce survivors. In this way large populations become resistant to insecticides. The more intensive and widespread the use of pesticides, the more rapidly the pests develop resistance.

The same problem has arisen with weeds. Chemical farming, dependent on the use of herbicides and pesticides, has increased with "no-till" farming, opening a vast new market for herbicides. As farmers eliminate the easy-to-kill weeds with an herbicide, more difficult-to-control weeds are becoming prevalent, causing an upward spiral in herbicide use.

GROUNDWATER

For decades, on the advice of chemical companies, farmers thought that pesticides would bind to the soil or break down into harmless chemicals. Either way, the thinking ran, they would not migrate from the location where they were applied. In 1979, aldicarb, a systemic pesticide, was discovered in Florida's aquifers; and DBCP, widely used to control nematodes (microscopic worms that attack plant roots), was found in California's groundwater, especially in the Central Valley. That same year, residues of aldicarb and its breakdown products were detected in more than 2,200 wells that draw water from the same aquifer underlying Long Island. Subsequently, aldicarb has been found in groundwater of at least fourteen other states. This finding came as a shock to the EPA because the manufacturer, Union Carbide, had predicted that aldicarb was short lived and would break down rapidly in the soil into harmless components. The fate of aldicarb, it turns out, is more complex.

Aldicarb is applied to the soil after the plant emerges for control of insects, nematodes, and mites. Some of the pesticide is absorbed by the plant roots into the plant as it grows. Pests are killed by the insecticide when they eat the plant leaves. Some aldicarb residues remain in the upper layer of soil, where they degrade. Excess water can carry aldicarb through the soil to groundwater; residues not broken down can move with groundwater to nearby streams or wells.

In a recent study of wells nationwide, the EPA found seventy-four different pesticides in the wells of thirty-eight states. Recent studies in Iowa have detected pesticides in half of that state's municipal wells.

FARM WORKER ILLNESS ———————————

The human health hazards of chemical-intensive agriculture are most acute for farm workers. They are exposed to pesticides in the fields in which they work, on the crops they cultivate and harvest, in the soil in which crops are grown, and on the drift of spray from adjoining fields and their own fields. Farm workers' homes abut agricultural fields and at times are downwind of pesticide spray. Pesticides migrate into the irrigation water and also into the wells that supply farm workers' homes. Farm workers are more likely to eat foods soon after they have been sprayed, so they probably eat more pesticides than the rest of the population. Finally, **agriculture is the only industry in the United States where children comprise a significant part of the work force.** Farm workers' occupational exposure to toxics begins at an earlier age than it does in the rest of us.

Statistics on sickness and death from exposure to pesticides underrate the hazard of these chemicals. In California, the only state that mandates physicians to report occupationally related pesticide illness, farm workers have the highest illness and injury rate of any workers. Even so, environmental health workers acknowledge that pesticide-related illness is severely underreported. Most medical personnel are not trained to recognize illness and injury due to pesticide exposure. Environmental physicians estimate that 300,000 cases of farm worker poisoning from pesticides occur annually in the United States.

PESTICIDES IN THE FOOD SUPPLY ———————

The entire picture of the hazards of pesticide use cannot be sketched for three reasons. The majority of pesticides have not been fully tested by the EPA for health hazards, so even if residues are found on food, we do not know the total health effects of eating those residues. The FDA tests 1 percent of our food for pesticide residues, so we do not know what the other 99 percent of untested food supply contains. And half of the pesticides applied to food cannot be detected by the routine laboratory methods the FDA uses, so many pesticides go untested on the tiny fraction of food that is tested.

A 1989 study conducted by the Natural Resources Defense Council on children's food consumption and pesticide residues in children's food, "Intolerable Risk: Pesticides in Our Children's Food," provides a valuable closeup look at pesticide residues in food supply and the inadequacy of pesticide regulation. The study found:

- On the average, a child is four times more exposed than an adult to eight widely used cancer-causing pesticides in food. These eight are only a fraction of the sixty-six potentially carcinogenic pesticides that may be found in a child's diet. Exposure to the eight pesticides in food alone may cause 6,200 children to develop cancer sometime in their lives.

- The greatest source of cancer risk found in this analysis was the residues of daminozide and its breakdown product, UDMH, in apples, apple products, and other foods.

- At least 17 percent of 18 million one- to five-year-olds are eating residues of neurotoxic organophosphate pesticides at levels above government-established "safe" levels in tomatos, tomato products, orange juice, and other foods. These pesticides poison the nervous systems of insects and, above certain levels, can damage the nervous systems of humans.

Children are least protected by the standards established for safe permissible residues on food, this report argues. They consume proportionately more fruit and vegetables, thus more pesticides, than do adults. Fruits, which make up a large proportion of a small child's diet, are the foods most likely to be contaminated by pesticide residues. Relative to body weight, the average preschool child

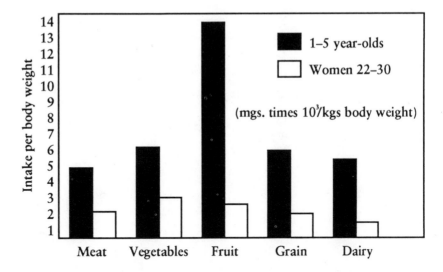

Figure 1.1 Food Intake: Children and Women

Reprinted with permission from *For Our Kids' Sake* published by Mothers & Others for
Pesticide Limits, a project of the Natural Resources Defense Council, 40 West 20th Street,
New York, NY 10011.

eats six times the amount of fruit and fruit products that an average
adult woman eats, and eighteen times the apple juice. Figures 1.1
and 1.2 compare the food consumption of women and children and
their relative exposure to pesticides.

Because of their physiology, young children may be more vulnerable to toxic effects of pesticides than adults. Because their nervous systems are still developing, they may be more susceptible to
neurotoxic pesticides than adults. Young children absorb more
toxic substances from their digestive systems than adults do, and
their vital organs may be more vulnerable to the toxic activity of
various compounds. The cells of infants and young children divide
more rapidly, which increases the probability that cell mutations
may be passed on to new cells. Therefore they are more at risk
from carcinogenic residues than adults. Finally, they are exposed
earlier and longer to toxic substances. For all these reasons, early
childhood is the period of a person's life when exposure to pesticide
residues is not only greatest in extent but also most critical in its
consequences.

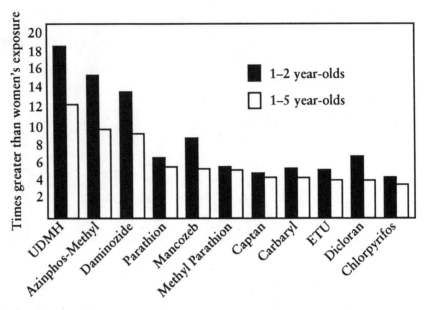

Figure 1.2 Differences in Relative Exposure (Children vs. Women)

Reprinted with permission from *For Our Kids' Sake* published by Mothers & Others for Pesticide Limits, a project of the Natural Resources Defense Council, 40 West 20th Street, New York, NY 10011.

Why Doesn't Regulation of Pesticides Protect Children?

Two federal agencies are charged to protect our food supply from unsafe levels of pesticides: the Environmental Protection Agency and the Food and Drug Administration. The programs of both agencies have gaping loopholes when it comes to protecting food supply from pesticide residues. In particular, the EPA's methods of setting safe limits leave children exposed to unsafe levels and quantities of pesticides in food.

First, the limits set by the EPA for allowable residues of pesticides are set by adult food consumption patterns, not children's. Therefore, the limits underestimate greatly the amount of pesticides eaten by children in their vegetable and fruit rich diets. Further, the estimates of what adults eat were based on food patterns in the late 1960s, which have substantially changed; people eat more fresh fruits and vegetables now than they did two decades ago. The NRDC calculates that children's consumption of cranberries is underestimated fourteenfold; grapes, sixfold; apples and oranges, fivefold; apricots, fourfold; strawberries, threefold; carrots and broccoli, twofold. As a result of not calculating children's food consumption and underestimating adults' consumption of fruits and vegetables, many of the maximum "acceptable" levels of pesticide residues set by the EPA are not safe for children. The NRDC estimates that if all preschool children were to eat the maximum allowable level of just three fungicides (captan, folpet, and mancozeb), more than 20,000 of these children would develop cancer in their lifetime as a result of exposure during preschool years.

These loopholes are not the only ones in a government program that is supposed to protect the national food supply but whose performance has been labeled a "record of neglect." Chapter 2 explains why.

RESOURCES

Reading/Information

Circle of Poison: Pesticides and People in a Hungry World (1981)
David Weir and Mark Schapiro
Institute for Food and Development Policy
145 Ninth St.
San Francisco, CA 94103
$3.95

Intolerable Risk: Pesticides in Our Children's Food (1989)
B. Sewell, R. Whyatt, J. Hathaway, and L. Mott
NRDC Publications Department
40 West 20th St.
New York, NY 10011
$25.00
Executive Summary available for $5.00

The Pesticide Conspiracy (1978)
Robert van den Bosch
Anchor Books

This book is out-of-print but remains an important resource. Possibly available in local libraries.

The Recurring Silent Spring (1989)
H. Patricia Hynes
Pergamon Press
Maxwell House Fairview Park
Elmsford, NY 10523
$27.50 hardcover, $12.95 paperback

Silent Spring (1962)
Rachel Carson
Houghton Mifflin
1 Beacon St.
Boston, MA 02108
25th Anniversary edition, 1987
$7.95 paperback

Chapter 2

Pesticide Regulations and Food Safety

*T*he federal pesticide programs ultimately ensure that pesticides are registered, marketed, and used, not that our food supply is free from pesticide residues. Even less do they help promote an agriculture that is ecologically sound and a food supply that is safe.

Harrison Wellford, an expert on chemicals and food safety, observed in 1972 that regulatory agencies betray the public trust less by what they do than by what they fail to do. He had in mind the twenty years that elapsed before the Pesticides Registration Division in the U.S. Department of Agriculture initiated its first action to recall a dangerous pesticide. In 1970, responsibility for registering pesticides was transferred from the Department of Agriculture to the newly created Environmental Protection Agency. The impetus for this transfer was Rachel Carson's exposé in *Silent Spring* of the mix of conflict of interest and negligence in the Department of Agriculture. The USDA, responsible for registering pesticides, had functioned as the major federal promoter of chemical pesticides through a series of broad-scale eradication programs such as the mass aerial spraying against the gypsy moth and the fire ant. In the case of the fire ant program, the mass aerial spraying of millions of acres with heptachlor and dieldrin was preceded by a publicity campaign in which the USDA distorted the impact of the fire ant in order to justify the pest control program. In the campaign to manipulate perception, an insect that was no more than a nuisance in Southern states was depicted as a menace to crops, livestock, and humans. The USDA showed complete ignorance of, or deliberate disregard for, the known toxicity of the poisons applied: Both were many times more toxic than DDT. Subsequently, the USDA cited the evidence of damage from their eradication campaigns, especially to domestic and wildlife, as exaggerated and misleading.

In 1972, Congress passed a new federal pesticide law to which amendments were added in 1975, 1978, and 1980. The new law and amendments were intended to make the registration process for chemical pesticides more rigorous by requiring industry to test chemical products for their potential to cause cancer, birth defects, and genetic mutations. The EPA could also require studies of the chemical's potential to dissolve in rainwater and contaminate groundwater, to accumulate in the food chain of the ecosystem, and so on. The EPA was given the authority to register all new pesticides before they could be sold and used as well as all new uses for already-existing pesticides. As for the thousands of pesticides already in use in 1972, they were to be reexamined and reregistered by the EPA as if they were new pesticides, since none had been tested by the new, more protective standards for their health and environmental effects. The EPA was further required to establish "tolerances," or allowable limits, of residues for pesticides that remain in or on food or animal feed. By law, the EPA was authorized to evaluate every pesticide in use, or proposed to be used, by weighing its benefits to agriculture against the harm caused by residues left on food that would be eaten by animals or humans or by residues left in the environment. Those pesticides judged to cause "unreasonable risk" or harm to humans or wildlife are to be restricted from use or banned altogether.

The EPA was given the formidable task of reviewing 35,000 pesticides in use when the 1972 law was passed, of establishing tolerances for every pesticide that left residues on food, and of registering new pesticides. In 1972, Congress mandated that the EPA complete reregistration by 1976. By 1978, Congress eliminated the deadline because it was uncertain how long this task of determining the safety of pesticides in use would take. Instead, the EPA was required to accomplish this work "as expeditiously as possible." The 1978 amendments also sanctioned a chemical-by-chemical rather than a product-by-product approach to the registration process. That is, the EPA could assess the approximately

600 basic active pesticide ingredients common to the now 50,000 pesticide products in lieu of evaluating each pesticide product. Also, the EPA established a special review process in 1975 that would enable the agency to conduct a rapid, detailed risk-benefit analysis of any pesticide in use that was found to be uniquely toxic. This process would enable the EPA to take rapid regulatory action, including canceling some or all uses; imposing use restrictions; and requiring labeling changes.

What does the record of pesticide regulation and protection of food supply look like? Recently, the EPA's pesticide program was studied by the Government Accounting Office at the request of Congress. This study found that the EPA has failed to evaluate the safety of the majority of chemical pesticides in use and those that remain as residues on food. At its current pace, the EPA will not finish its review and reassessment of the safety of pesticides in use until well into the twenty-first century. Until this review is completed, we will not know the full environmental and health risks of the 50,000 pesticides that are still in use, primarily in agriculture. New amendments to the pesticide law were passed in 1988 requiring the EPA to finish testing old pesticides within the next nine years. During this period the pesticides stay in use.

As of March 31, 1986, the EPA had not completed a single final reassessment on any of the 600 active pesticide ingredients. Preliminary assessments were completed on 124 of the active ingredients. This means that the data on a chemical were catalogued, data gaps were identified, and requests for missing or inadequate health and environmental studies were made to pesticide firms. Some restrictions were imposed on 60 percent of the 124 chemicals.

From the beginning of the special review program in 1975 through October 1985, the EPA completed thirty-two special reviews. As a result, five active ingredients were canceled for all uses; twenty-six active ingredients were restricted in use. The review process, intended to give a rapid review of chemicals found to be more toxic than originally realized, has generally taken two to six years; for some chemicals it has taken ten. During the period of review, the chemical stays in use and its uses can even be expanded; those most vulnerable to toxic substances—preschool children—can be eating it throughout their entire preschool years. The

NRDC calculates that the chemicals currently under special review constitute up to 98 percent of the cancer risk in food to the average preschool child.

The registration process is further complicated by the recognition that many so-called "inert" ingredients in pesticides—those chemicals added to affect the texture, solubility, and other physical characteristics—are themselves toxic, even if they don't kill target insects, weeds, or fungi. This finding was ignored when the EPA established a review method that examined active ingredients but overlooked inert ingredients. The EPA has identified 100 inert ingredients with known or suspected toxicity and another 800 for which there is insufficient toxicological data. Inert ingredients comprise the majority of the pesticide; they also remain in use while their hazard is undetermined.

Most scientists believe that there is no safe level of exposure to a carcinogen. Even so, the EPA has established allowable levels or tolerances for carcinogenic pesticides. This labeling is justified by a risk-benefit analysis that compares costs to growers and the economy against the risks of cancer to people. Allowing carcinogens into our food supply is based on the unpalatable cost-benefit calculation that puts a dollar price on human life and then compares the economic value of people who die from cancer as a result of carcinogens in the food supply to the economic value of the pesticides for the grower and manufacturer. **Yet no one has ever proven that pesticides are necessary to food supply, only that they are beneficial economically to manufacturers and growers.** The success of organic agriculture and integrated pest management proves that pesticides, as they are used in agriculture—as a first, not last, resort—are not necessary.

Thus far, we have discussed the EPA's failings in regulating pesticides: outdated calculations of pesticides in diet that grossly underestimate what children are exposed to, and a pesticide registration program that allows carcinogens to remain in the food supply and lags in examining the majority of pesticides for toxicity.

There is another component of the pesticide program: the monitoring of pesticide residues in food. The Food and Drug Administration monitors the food supply by collecting and analyzing a small sample of fruits, vegetables, dairy products, fish, processed foods, and animal feed each year for pesticide residues. The number of samples amounts to slightly more than 1 percent of imported produce, less than 1 percent of domestically grown produce, and less than 1 percent of the processed food that children eat—a limited sampling program, in other words. The tests used by the FDA can detect only 40 percent of the potential pesticides used on food. More typically, only 20 percent of the pesticides that can leave residues are tested for. For example, one-third of fruits and vegetables grown nationally are treated with a group of fungicides known as the EBDCs (ethylene bisdithiocarbamates), which the FDA has classified as a potentially high hazard. Yet EBDCs cannot be detected with the FDA's routine analysis, and only rarely is a special scan capable of detecting EBDCs used. Thus a limited overall sampling program is further limited by the number and types of analysis done routinely by the FDA. A Government Accounting Office study of the FDA's program found that the turnaround time for food analysis is so long that contaminated food is most likely to be sold and eaten by the time contamination is detected. In more than half the cases of violations, the food was never recovered. In only a few cases have growers been penalized.

Of all forms of pollution, pesticides in the food supply is the best-documented "record of neglect." But it is also an environmental problem with a well-laid-out path of solutions. In part, this is because agriculture is an ancient human activity: Some peoples have cultivated land for thousands of years without eroding or contaminating it. A legacy of sustainable agriculture, in other words, exists to draw on. There has always been a tradition of organic agriculture in the United States, although it has been trivialized as old fashioned and anachronistic. But organic agriculture has survived the stereotypes and is beginning to flourish. Recent advances in integrated pest management in agriculture schools and entomology departments offer chemical-based agriculture a way to come off chemical dependency and develop an increasingly biologically centered agriculture (see Chapter 3 for more on IPM). Finally, the United Farm Workers movement has kept the issues of farm worker safety in the fields and food safety in the grocery store on the bargaining table for thirty years. All of the more recent agricultural activism is undergirded by the most important chronicle of the environment in twentieth-century United States, *Silent Spring*, a book that indicted pesticides as a chemical assault on nature.

Because the path of solutions is well laid out before us, let us move onto it and consider the actions we can take.

RESOURCES

Guides to Action/Information

Americans for Safe Food
1501 16th St. NW
Washington, DC 20036

Center for Ecological Eating Education
1377 K St. NW, Suite 629
Washington, DC 20005
(202) 483-2616

Mothers and Others for Pesticide Limits
A Project of the Natural Resources Defense Council
P.O. Box 96641
Washington, DC 20090
(202) 783-7800

Launched successful grassroots campaign against Alar. Will expand to increase availablity of pesticide-free food in schools and communities, and to win congressional support for comprehensive reform of food safety laws and support of organic agriculture.

National Coalition Against Misuse of Pesticides
530 Seventh St. SE
Washington, DC 20003
(202) 543-5450

National coalition of grassroots organizations working on pesticide issues. Publishes newsletter, "Pesticides and You."

Rachel Carson Council, Inc.
8940 Jones Mill Rd.
Chevy Chase, MD 20815
(301) 652-1877

International resource center and clearinghouse on pesticide information.

Reading/Information

For Our Kids' Sake: How to Protect Your Child Against Pesticides in Food (1989)
Natural Resources Defense Council
P.O. Box 96641
Washington, DC 20090
$7.95

Pesticide Alert: A Guide to Pesticides in Fruits and Vegetables (1987)
Lawrie Mott and Karen Snyder
Natural Resources Defense Council
Sierra Club Books
730 Polk St.
San Francisco, CA 94109

Sowing the Wind (1972)
Harrison Wellford
Grossman Publishers
Not in print.

Chapter 3

Taking Action

Pesticide residues cannot be seen, smelled, or tasted in your fruits and vegetables, your meat, fish, and dairy products any more than most contaminants can in your drinking water. You can take immediate steps with food, however, to begin to ensure that pesticide residues are minimized in what you are serving and eating. First, take a look at our national food supply.

The Natural Resources Defense Council analyzed data from the FDA and California Department of Agriculture pesticide monitoring program, between 1982 and 1985. Over 110 different pesticides were detected in foods, some cancer causing. Two, DDT and dieldrin, were banned from use as far back as 1972 and 1974, respectively. They had either remained as residues in soil, since they are persistent chemicals, or were imported on food from countries that buy the chemicals from U.S. manufacturers. Not every pesticide in use was analyzed for, because the FDA routine scanning methods do not detect all pesticides. Even so, the FDA detected residues in 48 percent of twenty-six types of fruits and vegetables analyzed, a substantially higher percent than did California, because of more sensitive detection and the greater number of imported vegetables analyzed.

The NRDC found that certain fruits and vegetables are likely to contain pesticides more frequently than others, such as peaches, strawberries, and cherries, which are sprayed for cosmetic purposes; and foods with edible portions in contact with soil, such as celery and root crops. Some foods have natural barriers to some pesticide residues—corn husks and banana skins, for example. Consistently, imported foods contain more pesticide residues than domestic foods, a point we will revisit.

REDUCING THE RISK

Eat as usual: *bananas, corn, grapefruit, melons, oranges (for grated peel, buy organic or wash thoroughly)*

Wash well: *cabbage (discard outer leaves), cucumbers (peel if waxed), eggplant, peppers, tomatoes*

Wash thoroughly: *cauliflower, cherries, grapes, green beans, lettuce, potatoes, strawberries*

Special handling: *apples, pears and peaches (buy organic or IPM★; peel), broccoli and spinach (buy organic or IPM; cut or chop, place in water with some liquid dishwashing detergent, agitate, then rinse thoroughly), carrots (peel), celery (trim the leaves and top).*

SOURCE: Copyright 1989, CSPI. Reprinted from *Nutrition Action Healthletter* (1501 16th St. NW, Washington DC 20036 – 1499. $19.95 for 10 issues.

★Integrated pest management; see **Terms to Understand** p. 26.

What can you do to minimize pesticides in your home and community?

WHAT YOU CAN DO

1. Wash fruits and produce.

Some pesticide residues remain on the surface of the produce. Washing in water or a light detergent and water, rinsing well, and peeling will reduce residues. Although peeling does remove pesticides on the surface and in the skin, it often removes valuable nutrients and fiber as well. Some residues are absorbed through the produce skin and move to the edible tissue. Washing is not effective in these cases.

The Mothers and Others for Pesticide Limits campaign won a remarkable victory when the International Apple Institute announced in May 1989 that U.S. growers would stop using Alar on their crops, and Uniroyal Chemical Company decided in June 1989 to halt domestic sales of Alar. The campaign is now working for an immediate ban on *all* sales of Alar, including its export.

2. Buy domestically grown produce in season.

Perfect-looking produce recalls the adage: "All that glitters is not gold." Blemish-free fruit may mean that pesticides were used on it for cosmetic purposes. A shiny surface can signal a pesticide-impregnated wax. Many health advocates advise buying domestically grown produce in season, because imported produce generally contains more pesticide residues than domestically grown fruits and vegetables. They also caution that developing countries do not have sufficiently stringent pesticide regulations.

In fairness to developing countries, I would warn that the circle of poison that returns pesticides to us in imported food, begins in the United States. The U.S. pesticide law allows U.S. pesticide manufacturers to manufacture for sale in developing countries pesticides that are banned in the United States. The sale of pesticides in developing countries was introduced through multinational companies in quest of markets and international aid agencies promoting models of Western agriculture. Pesticides often come hand in glove with agricultural aid packages. Not buying the produce of developing countries protects the individual, but it does not address the issue of exporting pesticide poisons. These poisons constitute one of the major health hazards to women and children in developing countries because they comprise a majority of agricultural labor.

3. Buy organically grown produce.

In March 1989, a major wholesale distributor of organic produce in the northeastern United States declared that a transformation of agriculture is taking place. Sales of organic produce quadrupled in just that month. California's Certified Organic Farmers Association has 32,000 acres in organic agriculture, a quadrupling in four years. According to their promotional literature, all 116 Stop and Shop stores now sell organic produce.

The demand for organic produce is high. But the supply is tight because switching back to organic farming methods means building up organic material in the soil and an indigenous population of beneficial insects—a process that takes one to five years. In addition, many states require that soil be free of pesticides for three years before the produce grown on it can be sold as "certified or-

---

TERMS TO UNDERSTAND

More and more signs are going up over produce shelves in the supermarket, but what do they mean? There's a rapidly developing lexicon for what's organic and what's not, as follows:

Certified organically grown: No pesticides, fungicides, ripening agents (such as Alar). No chemical fertilizers used. The farm has been inspected by a state-authorized certifying agency.

Transitional organic or transorganic: Grown on a farm which has not completed its certification process (in most states, three years is required). No pesticides, ripening agents or other chemicals used, but residues may persist in the soil.

IPM (integrated pest management): Natural insect repellents and pest control methods are used; chemical fertilizers are rarely used. Tiny amounts of insecticide sprays may be applied in an emergency, especially on fruits that are difficult to grow without insecticides. However, no ripening agents are applied.

Ecological: The same as IPM.

SOURCE: "Organics Explosion," *The Valley Advocate*, Hatfield, MA, 1989.
Courtesy of Kathy Stoddard.

---

ganic." With high demand and tight supply, already expensive organic produce may become pricier. Also, as one writer pointed out, the fact that organic produce may not look different from other produce (except for some blemishes) makes this industry a likely breeding ground for fraud.

Nancy Greenspan, a member of the Rachel Carson Council Board of Directors, asks every business and organization that she supports or patronizes what pesticide measures they employ. She makes it clear that if they rely on unsuitable toxic chemicals, she may cancel her business with them. She found that a local grocer who sells as much uncontaminated produce as possible had an exterminator come in monthly to spray the store and produce areas. At Greenspan's advice, the grocer spoke with the person who was responsible for changing pesticide use in county schools and introduced a new integrated pest management (IPM) program into his store to minimize use of pesticides.

❑ ❑ ❑

4. Grow your own.

Since the first food gatherers began to collect and plant seeds, human beings have farmed and grown their own food. In many parts of the world, people still grow much of their own food and supplement what they grow and raise with what they buy and trade at market. Only in this century did people in industrial countries become so separated from their food sources that most of us grew up thinking of food as coming from supermarkets, like cars come from a car dealer, without a clue to the sources and the processes that produce our food. In the 1970s, victory gardens, begun during World War II, were revived and expanded. At the same time, most U.S. cities started community garden projects. Interest in working with soil and growing our own food was rekindled.

❑ ❑ ❑

A carpenter whose sole garden space is flower boxes on the wall of his lower Beacon Hill, Boston shop described for me his system of composting to make soil for his vegetable and flower garden and grape vines:

Last year I started composting in a large, plastic, household-size trash can—indoors, since I have no yard. Everything trimmed from the garden or left over from the kitchen goes in. Sawdust from the shop (but not plywood, because of the glues) gets added when the mixture gets too liquid or stinky, this regulates it amazingly. It gets turned to mix, otherwise it requires no attention. One barrel is good for a year, one full and very heavy barrel. In the spring, the stuff gets worked into the soil. So it *is* possible to do this in the city, and with less effort than throwing out the garbage . . . you never have to take the can out.

And on Martha's Vineyard, Solviva blooms. Named for a marigold-like Swedish flower, Solviva is a 3,000-square-foot greenhouse with a two-layered polyester glazing designed and tended by Swedish-born Anna Edey. Attached rabbit hutches are a source of heat, carbon dioxide, and compost. Inside the greenhouse, elevated growing tubes enable Edey to grow enough food to do a profitable business selling organic produce to restaurants. Her integrated approach to pest management includes a canopy of nasturtiums, plates of beer for slugs, isopods, and the predatory ladybird beetles. Edey is convinced that community greenhouses hold great potential for growing local food.

❏ ❏ ❏

5. Tend Your Lawn Without Chemicals.

The agriculture industry is the largest user of pesticides, but homeowners account for a large percentage of pesticide use. One environmental group estimates that 40 percent of pesticide products on the market are for home use. The National Academy of Sciences finds that homeowners use approximately 85 million pounds of pesticides per year. If we assume that much of this is used for lawn care, it amounts to 5–10 pounds per acre, per year, a rate of application to suburban lawns which exceeds that applied to other land areas in the country.

One garden aficionado describes the quest for the perfect lawn as a specific and recent American tradition. The lawn, he says, is to Americans what gardens are to the English. Flower and vegetable gardens are designed at the edges and borders as a frame for the centerpiece lawn. If this is true, writes Warren Schultz of Rodale Press in *Chemical-Free Lawn*, then we should think of and understand our lawn, with its varieties of grasses, insects, weeds and diseases, as we do our gardens. Herbicides kill weeds but also some lawn grasses. Herbicides and other pesticides kill beneficial earthworms, spiders, and mites, which help control weeds, bugs, and fungi. Water-soluble nitrogen fertilizer can end up feeding weeds more than grass. Lawns are ecosystems as much as gardens, he writes, and can be tended with organic methods much like gardens.

But another issue swims to the surface here. Underlying the quest for a perfect lawn—a desire largely stirred up by the advertising of lawn care chemical companies—is a limiting attitude toward

Figure 3.1 Garden of a Beacon Hill Handyman
Courtesy of Steve Bastide.

unwanted plants called "weeds." As a child in the 1950s, I remember being shocked when my father picked a "weed," rubbed it to elicit its fragrance, and had me and my sisters taste it—wild spearmint! Another time he ate dandelion leaves plucked right from the plant, called them "salad greens," and talked about vitamin C. We thought he had strange tastes. Mainly I hoped he didn't behave like this in front of friends. This was the era when my school friends were moving to the newly built suburbs with color-coded, split-level houses and grass-perfect American lawns.

Now I am not so naive to reclaim poison ivy along with wild

mint and dandelions. But haven't you, like me, rediscovered the beauty of swaths of diverse wildflowers and ferns along roadsides and patches of mixed groundcovers like vinca and lily of the valley in place of homogeneous grass, so that the "perfect lawn" now looks bland and synthetic? And yes, I have been known to collect dandelion greens for salad.

RIGHT TO KNOW

Many states are considering requiring—and some already do—commercial landscaping companies and private homeowners to post warning notices on lawns when they apply pesticides and herbicides as part of lawncare. Scotts Turfbuilder Plus 2 contains herbicides such as 2,4-D, one of the constituents of Agent Orange. The commercial names of these chemicals do not inform people of their chemical hazards. But the signs do, warning parents to keep pets and children away from treated areas for 48 to 72 hours. But robins eating earthworms that have ingested lawn chemicals can't read the notices, nor can animals wandering through the treated areas. Nor can preschool and illiterate children.

❏ ❏ ❏

Thirty years ago June Larson moved from Chicago to the small town of Wauconda because her daughter had muscular dystrophy and needed to be kept away from exposure to chemicals in the urban environment. In Chicago, her daughter had once been hospitalized for severe exposure to DDT. In Wauconda, Larson threatened to sue the state when her daughter was exposed to pesticides sprayed along a local highway to control mosquitos. Larson next worked for an ordinance that residents be notified when lawn care chemicals were used. In September 1984, the town passed a precedent-setting ordinance requiring lawn care companies to obtain permits from the town and to post notices before spraying, banning application in wind over 10 miles per hour, and limiting spraying along a common property line. The lawn care companies sued the town and tied up the ordinance in court, complaining about a "chemophobic whirlwind." Meanwhile the ordinance has served as a model for the many right-to-know laws that have subsequently been passed by state and local legislatures.

❑ ❑ ❑

The right-to-know law is extremely controversial, threatening businesses, farmers, and individuals who depend on or are intent on using pesticides. It has acted as a deterrent for farmers and homeowners, who have stopped using chemicals rather than posting their property and taking the grief from neighbors. **If you are interested in working for such a law in your state or town, see the Resources section.**

TAKE ACTION IN YOUR COMMUNITY

1. Support IPM for Mosquito and Other Insect Control.

Most mosquito control programs rely on chemicals like malathion to kill mosquitos. To be effective, malathion must be applied once or twice a week. It is toxic to fish, bees, and many other beneficial insects. Where it is frequently used, entire populations of mosquitos have become resistant. Pesticides should be used as a last resort, not a first, for two compelling reasons: (1) They are not discriminating in their toxicity, and (2) insects can develop resistance to them, rendering them ineffective.

The Massachusetts Audubon Society encourages use of pesticides to control mosquitos only if a public emergency exists. Under most conditions, other methods developed by researchers in integrated pest management (IPM) are much more preferable. For example, a bacterium, *Bacillus thuringiensis* (Bt), kills mosquito larvae with minimal environmental damage. The Massachusetts Middlesex Mosquito Control District uses "Open Marsh Water Management" to minimize pools of stagnant salt water, the breeding site for the salt marsh mosquito. This principle can be applied at home. Empty water from old flower pots, old tires, children's toys, cans or bottles, water cans, or buckets—all potential breeding grounds of mosquitos. The same is true for clogged roof gutters, water troughs, poorly maintained sumps, overirrigated lawns and fields, plastic wading pools, and bird baths. These tips, says Audubon, may take care of 50 percent of the problem. A neighborhood project would be more effective.

Audubon's tollfree Environmental Helpline number for mosquito control is listed in Resources.

❑ ❑ ❑

In his book *The Pesticide Conspiracy*, the prominent entomologist Robert van den Bosch described an early, successful IPM mosquito control strategy. Marin County, California has a 2,000-acre wetland, Petaluma Marsh, which had been a major mosquito breeding ground. As a consequence, much of the marsh was aerially sprayed with the pesticide parathion five times a year. The county entomologist responsible for mosquito control deduced that the mosquito source was not the natural wetland waterways that are flushed daily by tides but the "potholes" created when the area was used as a practice bombing range by the military during World War II. The potholes did not drain with tidal flushing, and their stagnating water became ideal breeding sites for mosquitos. A pothole drainage system was designed that permits daily flushing. As a result, aircraft stopped spraying the marshes with pesticides. The mosquito problem has disappeared from nearby communities: Dairy farmers reported their herds are free of mosquito swarms for the first time in memory.

In September 1989, after a summer of studying the cause of the unexpected decline in the gypsy moth population in Connecticut, two entomologists from the U.S. Department of Agriculture concluded that the credit goes to a fungus. Varieties of the fungus occur naturally in Europe and Japan, where gypsy moth infestations are not a problem as they are in the United States. The fungus was imported from Japan in 1909 and released in 1910 in several suburbs of Boston. Although the experiment was thought to be a failure, the USDA entomologists concluded that the original fungus spread unnoticed thoughout the northeastern U.S. and controlled a gypsy moth outbreak in 1989.

❑ ❑ ❑

2. *Petition Your Supermarket to Sell Organic Food.*

Already many supermarket chains, such as Stop and Shop, have started to stock organic produce, the result in great part of the tremendous publicity given to pesticide residues in food during the Alar campaign. Encourage your local supermarket to carry organic food or expand the organic food section by using a basic organizing strategy. Circulate a petition asking that the store offer certified pesticide-free produce. Give it to the produce manager and send a copy to corporate management, adding that you will shop where organic produce is available if they don't offer it. Assist your supermarket manager in finding growers and wholesalers of organic produce. Here is a sample petition developed by Mothers and Others for Pesticide Limits that the campaign encourages you to copy and use.

PETITION FOR PESTICIDE-FREE FOOD

Dear supermarket manager:

As regular customers in your store, we are concerned about pesticide residues in food. In particular, we are disturbed by the findings of a recent study by the Natural Resources Defense Council showing that our children are being exposed to dangerous levels of pesticides in their food. Therefore, we request that your supermarket locate suppliers of pesticide-free food and make it available in your store. Other supermarkets across the country are offering certified organic produce for sale. We urge you to do the same.

Signed   Address

_____

_____

_____

SOURCE: Reprinted with permission from *For Our Kid's Sake* published by Mothers and Others for Pesticide Limits, a project of the Natural Resources Defense Council, 40 West 20th Street, New York, NY 10011.

---

3. Support the UFW Grape Boycott.

The first meeting to organize migrant farm workers into what would become the United Farm Workers (UFW) movement was convened by Cesar Chavez in an abandoned theater in Fresno, California on September 30, 1962, three days after the publication of *Silent Spring*. In September 1965, farm workers walked out of grape orchards in Delano, California because of unsafe pesticide exposure, unsanitary working conditions, and poverty-level wages. One result of this historic action was a ban on the use of DDT, dieldrin, and aldrin in the first contracts with grape growers. The ban on pesticide use proved to be the most controversial element of the agreement signed in 1970, after a five-year strike-boycott of table and wine grapes by the United Farm Workers. Growers held out longer on the contract clause banning the use of these three pesticides than on any other demand. The United Farm Workers won the ban two years before the EPA would rule on DDT.

In assessing the gains farm workers have made over the past three decades, Chavez points out that even though there have been some economic benefits won, one aspect of farm work has worsened: the use of toxic pesticides. In 1985, the UFW called for a new boycott on fresh table grapes from California until the grape industry would agree to three conditions:

1. A ban on five pesticides used in growing grapes: captan, parathion, phosdrin, dinoseb, and methyl bromide.
2. A joint and well-publicized UFW/grower testing program for pesticide residues on grapes sold in stores.
3. Free and fair elections for farm workers and good-faith collective bargaining.

Grapes are the largest crop in California. They receive more restricted-use pesticide applications than any other fresh food crop, approximately 8 million pounds of more than 130 different pesticides. Most of the pesticides used have not been fully tested to determine whether they cause cancer, birth defects, chronic effects, sterility, or damage to genetic material. Approximately one-third of them are suspected or proven carcinogens. More than half of all acute pesticide-related illness in California involves cultivating or harvesting grapes. Each of the five pesticides named in the boycott is extremely toxic; some have caused extensive worker poisoning and illness; some are known carcinogens; some leave residues on grapes. The boycott is still on. Thus far, food chains in Manhattan, Massachusetts, and Canada have agreed to stop carrying California table grapes.

❏ ❏ ❏

Pheromones, which are natural sex attractants, are a safe, biological alternative to chemical pesticides. The pheromones from the female grape berry moth can be duplicated to confuse the male moth so that they are unable to mate and produce larvae that damage vineyards. In New York state vineyards, Cornell University entomologists have found that placing small amounts of pheromones per acre in the spring can provide excellent control of the grape berry moth throughout the summer. Pheromones have the potential to replace up to 1,000 tons of chemical pesticides in New York vineyards each year. Pheromones work not because they are toxic to the target insect but because they disrupt the reproductive cycle. They are naturally produced by insects, can be added by farmers, dissipate rapidly in the environment, and leave no harmful residues on crops. Pheromones are one example of a biological control in integrated pest management.

❏ ❏ ❏

ECOLOGICAL AGRICULTURE: INTEGRATED PEST MANAGEMENT

The linchpin in the defense of the new synthetic pesticides was that they would protect agriculture from severe crop loss caused by insect pests. A research entomologist for more than three decades and professor at the University of California, Berkeley, Robert van den Bosch confirmed in field studies, his own and others, that the opposite was true. He verified that chemical-intensive agriculture does not control pests, it creates them. It also places an immense financial burden on farmers who become caught on a treadmill of increasing pesticide use due to rapid insect resistance.

Van den Bosch proposed shifting insect pest control from the "poisoning of things" to a holistic, ecologically based strategy of minimizing insect damage to crops and disease-bearing insects. Called integrated pest managment or IPM, this alternative strategy relies on careful crop and insect monitoring to detect when pesticide applications will have the optimum effect so as to minimize their use; cultural practices such as crop rotation to help break the pest's reproductive cycle; biological controls, like the pheromones, to confuse the male grape berry moth; and the use of cover crops and plant varieties that resist pests. The example of solving mosquito control by designing a drainage system for potholes with standing water is an example of an IPM solution.

A Northampton, Massachusetts farmer, James Syznal, recently invented the Beetle Eater, a vacuum cleaner – type machine that removes Colorado potato beetles by blowing air up from the bottom of potato plants while a suction device vacuums the bugs from the top. The Beetle Eater sells for $30,000, an amount that can be saved in one growing season by eliminating pesticide spraying on a 300-acre potato farm.

There has always been an agriculture based on sustaining nature—soil fertility, beneficial insects, and soil organisms—rather than controlling nature with toxic pesticides or the replacement of nature with synthetic fertilizers and pesticides. Called variably organic agriculture and sustainable agriculture, it is, as I see it, the standard to which integrated pest management should aspire. The value of IPM is that it offers farmers caught in the pesticide treadmill a way to slow down the intensive use of synthetic pesticides with no initial losses (they enjoy gains, in fact, through savings on expensive pesticides) and to restore more biologically sound methods of growing food. As Rachel Carson wrote: "The earth's vegetation is part of a web of life . . . Sometimes, we have no choice but to disturb these relationships, but we should do so thoughtfully, with full awareness that what we do may have consequences remote in time and place."

RESOURCES

Guides to Action/Organizations

See Resources in Chapters 1 and 2 for information on organizing against pesticides in food.

Audubon Hotline for Mosquito Control
800 541-3443

Bio-Integral Resource Center (BIRC)
P.O. Box 7414
Berkeley, CA 94707

Publishes *The Common Sense Pest Control Quarterly* and *The IPM Practitioner*

Information on alternative control of pests in home and garden.

The Chemical-Free Lawn
Warren Schultz
Rodale Press
See address and phone under *The New Farm*
$14.95 paper, $21.95 cloth

Integrated Pest Management (IPM)

The county Cooperative Extension Service in your state may have an IPM program with publications on results. The Massachusetts Cooperative Extension Service has an extensive IPM program with Massachusetts growers, undertaken in 1978. Their publications document methods and results.

Cooperative Extension Service
Stockbridge Hall
University of Massachusetts
Amherst, MA 01003

Integrated Pest Management Manual for Turf
Waltham Field Station
240 Beaver St.
Waltham, MA 02154

International Alliance for Sustainable Agriculture
1701 University Ave. SE, Room 202
Minneapolis, MN 55414
(612) 331-1099

Right-to-Know Ordinance

Rachel Carson Council, Inc.
8940 Jones Mill Rd.
Chevy Chase, MD 20815
(301) 652-1877

For sample ordinance language and information on how to initiate a right-to-know ordinance in your municipality or state.

United Farm Workers

National Farm Workers Health Group
P.O. Box 22579
San Francisco, CA 94122
(415) 731-6569

"Wrath of Grapes" Boycott Information and Support
United Farm Workers of America, AFL-CIO
La Paz
Keene, CA 93570
(805) 822-5571

Reading/Information

The New Farm, *Organic Gardening*, and *Prevention* magazines
Rodale Press and Research Center
33 E. Minor St.
Emmaus, PA 18098
(215) 967-5171
Offer a wealth of information on alternative agriculture.

PART TWO

Solid Waste: Treasure in Trash

*Recycling is better than disposal, reuse is better than recycling, but re-
duction is the best of all.*

Donella H. Meadows, Dartmouth College
(1989)

*I*n the verdant, seaward city of Seattle, I listened to Mayor
Charles Royer describe the premier recycling program in the
country. In less than two years, Seattle has achieved 30 percent recycling of household waste. The city's goal is 60 percent by 1994.
Also in the audience were more than 300 local officials from cities
and counties that face common solid waste problems: a growing
volume of trash; no more than a few years' additional capacity in
existing landfills; active landfills shut down because they are leaching toxic materials; and organized citizen opposition to new landfills and incinerators. The participants came to this conference on
recycling, sponsored by the National League of Cities, because recycling is no longer an issue of "if" and "when," as one speaker
put it; it is a matter of "must" and "how."

Before I left for the conference, a friend confessed that when she
hears the term "solid waste," she never knows whether it refers to
shit or old tires. In the waste world, solid waste is whatever you put
out in the trash for collection or take to the landfill. Solid waste en-
compasses paper, food and yard waste, disposable diapers, plastics,
bottles and beverage containers, tires, metal, appliances, mat-
tresses, and furniture. It includes commercial, office, and light industrial waste, the majority of which is corrugated cardboard,
paper, and plastic.

Much solid waste can be recycled and reused for the same or
new purposes; some can be composted for gardens and landscaping; some can be repaired and resold. Recycling and reuse are a
kind of modern alchemy in which one person's scrap becomes another's valuable raw material. How much treasure is there in trash?
The most optimistic estimate from government officials of how

much of our waste can be recycled is about 60 percent. This calculation comes at a point when serious recycling programs are only two to three years old and the premier programs have so far achieved 30 percent. As recycling becomes a universal way of handling waste, as markets are aggressively developed for recycled products, and as people *demand* that new products and packaging be recyclable, the estimate of how much of our waste can be recycled will probably climb. **Some environmentalists contend that 70 to 90 percent of our waste can be reused and recycled.**

Recycling lends itself to anecdotes and stories—whether it is a proud city official talking about color-coded curbside containers or a personal story of reorganizing a space-tight kitchen for separate glass, metal, and paper containers. At the recycling conference a mayor from Kentucky asked the mayor of Seattle if it were true that the Seattle zoo composts the manure of herbivorous animals and offers it free to gardeners as "Zoo Doo." (It does.) Elsewhere a woman told of trying to fool the system when recycling was first introduced into her town. She has a small kitchen, and the notion of setting aside separate containers for newspapers, cans, bottles, and mixed paper other than newspaper was overwhelming. She felt she would be living in a garbage dump. To avoid recycling, she bought extra thick plastic bags so that the trash collector wouldn't notice the newspapers crumpled up inside. She packed empty aluminum cans into milk cartons, then stuffed the cartons so they wouldn't rattle. After a few months she realized that it now took her more time to disguise the trash than it would to separate it for recycling, so she devised a recycling closet with separate storage bins for newspapers, glass, and cans. Not only has separating the trash become second nature for everyone in her household, but they have become more conscious of shopping and buying in an environmentally sound way. They purchase milk in paper cartons, not nonrecyclable plastic jugs. They avoid takeout food wrapped in styrofoam. They save brown paper bags and reuse them at the supermarket.

I called recycling "modern" alchemy. In fact, it is an old tradition that was abandoned more than thirty years ago. During World War I, the Depression, and World War II, recycling was commonplace for households, businesses, and garbage collectors in the

United States. Children recycled bottles and scrap materials for their spending money. Until the early 1960s, "shirt hospitals" in New York City refit old collars to new shirts. One story has it that when Los Angeles mayor Sam Yorty ran for office in the late 1950s, he campaigned for an end to separating recyclables in garbage.

The roots of the current recycling movement, however, are firmly set in the late 1960s and early 1970s grassroots environmental movement. Within six months of Earth Day, April 22, 1970—a day of national consciousness awakening about pollution and the environment—more than 3,000 community-based recycling centers were created. Many of these centers closed during the recession of 1974–1975 because tax policies favored new materials over recycled ones. Leaders in the current recycling movement, however, "cut their teeth," as one puts it, in that early grassroots recycling movement. And extensive educational materials produced at that time for schools, communities, and media form the database for today's public awareness programs.

By 1980, local public officals began to feel the squeeze in waste as municipal landfills filled up and new ones became nearly impossible to site. Municipal solid waste managers turned to a combination of recycling and incineration, with low expectations, however, for recycling—20 to 30 percent of the waste stream—and great expectations for incinerators—all the rest of it. Environmentalists saw this strategy as one that favored incinerators, because recycling to separate out the nonburnables—glass and metal—merely smooths the way for incineration.

The later 1980s has witnessed a rapid, radical change in solid waste strategy and management plans. Citizen groups have arisen to stop incinerators from being planned or built until waste reduction, reuse, and recycling are fully implemented to their maximum potential. In Sonoma County, California, the county waste management plan calls incineration unnecessary and politically unacceptable. Nor can incineration solve the problem of landfills with less than four to five years' operating capacity. A new incinerator will take at least that long to build *without* community protest and permit difficulties. On the other hand, a comprehensive community-based recycling program can be fully implemented in one year.

At the Seattle conference, regional solid waste planners talked nonchalantly about the goal of 60 percent recycling when many had accepted a 20 to 30 percent goal only a few years ago. By 1995, when front-running cities will be recycling more than half of their waste stream, what will the planners' new estimate be?

Recycling the materials we use—almost all of which come from the Earth as raw materials, and some of which are extremely polluting when disposed—is *living as if the Earth matters*. Every ton of material that is reused saves from 1.5 to 3 tons of new materials. Reusing finished products reduces industrial pollution from manufacturing and pollution from waste incineration. Recycling rather than landfilling or incinerating is also living as if people and local economies mattered. The Washington-based Institute for Local Self-Reliance calculates that recycling creates thirty-six jobs for every 10,000 tons of materials recycled compared to six jobs per 10,000 tons brought to a traditional disposal facility. On the average, it costs $30 per ton to recycle waste, $50 per ton to landfill waste, and $65 to $75 per ton to incinerate. Thus recycling can transform the local waste economy into a productive sector and save local governments enormous waste disposal costs.

In many cases, we are being brought to recycling by a crisis rather than by an ideal, which is what the Director of Seattle Solid Waste Utility says impelled her city to move so quickly. But the Chinese *kanji* for "crisis," Diana Gale told us, is made up of two characters, one meaning "danger" and the other meaning "opportunity." In Seattle, a crisis—existing landfills were placed on the EPA's national list of hazardous waste sites and shut down—was turned into an opportunity: an ambitious recycling program. For the people of Seattle who pay directly for garbage collection, abruptly rising garbage fees prompted enormous participation in the recycling program. To promote the program, Seattle restructured garbage rates and shared the savings from recycling with residents. In 1988, the city paid haulers $48 per ton for recycled materials, half the cost per ton Seattle would pay for new landfill space. That same year residents normally paid $18.55 a month to have two cans of refuse picked up by the city. If they separated out paper, glass, and aluminum cans from their garbage in containers provided by the city's contractors and reduced their garbage to one can, they paid $13.55. Superrecyclers are offered the option of an even cheaper minican. To minimize their weekly nonrecyclable garbage, Seattle officials said, people are inclined to buy soda in recyclable cans and to avoid unnecessary packaging in products they purchase. Built into this recycling program is the incentive to reduce waste before recycling it. With new programs to process yard waste into compost and recycle certain plastics, Seattle expects to attain its goal of 60 percent recycling by 1994.

Recycling, as many people testify, often brings about a change in consciousness. First, people begin to take note, then they resent how excessive packaging has become. They observe the "creep" in plastic replacing metal, glass, and paper containers as well as packaging materials. They reuse materials before throwing them away or recycling them. They avoid unnecessary waste and choose recyclable, returnable, and biodegradable products over disposable one. Surveys of households involved in curbside recycling show that once they recycle regularly, people reduce their waste by 20 percent above and beyond what they recycle. Whether they are brought to recycling by a crisis or an ideal, many agree that, once there, they enjoy a different kind of satisfaction—one that comes with "walking softly on this Earth."

RESOURCES

Reading/Information

"Mining Urban Wastes: The Potential for Recycling" (1987)
Cynthia Pollack
Worldwatch Paper 76
$4

"Material Recycling: The Virtue of Necessity" (1983)
William U. Chandler
Worldwatch Paper 56
$4

The Worldwatch Institute
1776 Massachusetts Ave. NW
Washington, DC 20036
(202) 452-1999

"The United States Recycling Movement, 1968 to 1986" (1986)
Neil Seldman
Institute for Local Self-Reliance
2425 18th St. NW
Washington, DC 20009
(202) 232-4108
$6.50

Chapter 4

Defining the Problem

The United States creates about 450,000 tons of residential and commercial solid waste every day. By the year 2000, this amount is expected to reach 530,000 tons per day. What happens to the half million tons of daily trash? Today, 80 percent of our waste is buried in landfills. The Environmental Protection Agency estimates that in the next five to ten years more than twenty-seven states and half of the country's cities will run out of landfill space. Major cities including New York and Los Angeles will exhaust their landfill space in just a few years; Philadelphia and others have no more. Of the remaining 20 percent of waste that is not landfilled, 10 percent is recycled and 10 percent is incinerated.

Let us make these enormous quantities personal by looking at the amount and kind of waste generated by you, the "average person," in a year (Figure 4.1).

The United States is glibly called a "throwaway" society. **This is not just because Americans generate and throw away nine times as much waste as does a person in Africa or Central America; but also because we generate two to three times the amount of waste as people living in industrial countries with a comparable or better standard of living.** The amount of trash per person and per household in the United States steadily increased from 1960 through 1980, with packaging a growing component of trash. On the average, packaging accounts for 13 percent of food costs and 50 percent of garbage costs. Nor do we recycle our waste as well as many industrial countries. In Sweden, one-fourth of all solid waste is composted. Japan and the Netherlands collect more than half their aluminum, paper, and glass for recycling.

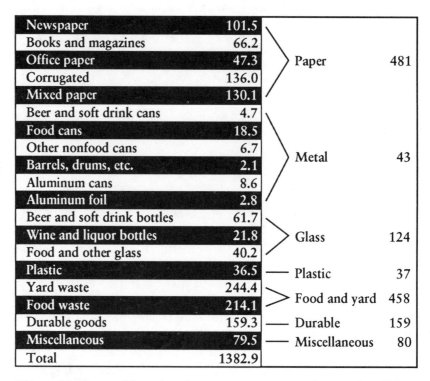

Figure 4.1 Composition of trash per person, per year, in pounds, 1985
SOURCE: Massachusetts Department of Environmental Management.

Often the crisis in solid waste is better captured by images than in words or numbers:

- Stockpiled tires on fire and burning for months

- Community protests over siting new incinerators and new landfills

- Abandoned refrigerators and appliances littering the landscape as disposal becomes more costly and landfills refuse these "white goods"

- Landfills rising like skyscrapers to dominate the local skyline—sometimes becoming the highest point in their locality—because new space is scarce

The mess we are in with solid waste was best dramatized by the now-legendary picture of the wandering garbage-laden barge that circled the world for two years in quest of a dumpsite and ultimately returned to New York Harbor, still garbage laden and garnished with a banner, "NEXT TIME . . . TRY RECYCLING—Greenpeace." But the barges and ships once piled with U.S. waste that return empty, having dumped their waste in developing countries or at sea, are far more worrisome.

NEXT TIME . . . TRY RECYCLING

Aluminum

Aluminum, especially in cans, is very valuable. It takes 95 percent less energy to produce an aluminum can from an existing one than from ore. The Aluminum Association reports that aluminum can recycling in 1987 saved enough energy to supply residential electricity to New York City for over six months. The industry has the capacity to purchase and process all the aluminum in the country. Cans are the most common form of recyclable aluminum. Aluminum siding, gutters, downspouts, storm door and window frames, lawn furniture frames, and the like are also recyclable. A magnet that attracts iron and steel but not aluminum can be used to ensure that a material is aluminum.

Iron and Steel

Iron and steel are the most recycled materials used today. Scrap metal dealers have also been the most visible recyclers, doing business many years before recent comprehensive recycling programs. In whatever form we use steel—pipes, automobiles, or tin food cans—it is recyclable. Tin food containers are recycled by separating the tin, an expensive imported metal, from the steel in the can. High-grade tin is recovered for new tin products, and steel is sold for reprocessing as new steel for manufacturing.

Paper

Waste paper is the largest component of the waste stream, com-

Connecticut is the first state to require that newspapers use recycled paper as a fixed percentage of their newsprint. By 1993, publishers of in-state papers and out-of-state papers with a Connecticut circulation of more than 40,000 must use recycled paper for 20 percent of production; by 1998, for 90 percent of production.

Florida has imposed a fee and credit system on publishers to encourage use of recyled paper. A publisher pays a 10¢ waste recovery fee for every ton of new newsprint used and receives a 10¢ credit for every ton of recycled newsprint used.

prising about 40 percent. Five broad grades of waste paper are recycled: newspaper, corrugated cardboard, office paper, mixed paper, and high-grade waste paper. Newspapers constitute the majority of recycled used paper. About 25 percent of newsprint is recovered for recycling, mainly for new newsprint. A major portion is sold to foreign markets, such as Canada, Italy, West Germany, Mexico, and South Korea. Office paper represents a relatively new grade of waste paper as offices implement recycling programs. Ledger and computer paper are higher grades of paper fiber and can be recycled to manufacture new paper products, such as writing paper, computer paper, and paper towels. High-grade waste paper is generated by commercial printers in clipping waste. Mixed paper is one of the largest components of residential waste, including cereal boxes, junk mail, telephone books, paper packaging, and grocery bags. Because it is made of a mix of low-grade papers, many paper recycling programs do not accept mixed paper with newspapers and high-grade office paper. There is a strong export market for mixed paper, however, especially in Japan, Taiwan, and South Korea.

We hear increasingly of a glut in the recycled newspaper market. The problem may lie with U.S. newspaper publishers: Few print on recycled paper and they oppose legislation requiring its use.

Glass

Glass comprises about 10 percent of our waste stream; all container glass is recyclable. The primary components of glass are materials that are easy to procure and in abundant supply—sand, soda ash, and limestone. Crushed glass or cullet, however, melts at a lower temperature than the raw materials and thus requires less energy in the production of new glass containers. Used glass bottles and jars are collected and remelted with raw materials to make new glass containers. The Glass Packaging Institute reports that 25 percent of any given glass container is made from recycled glass.

Plastics

Plastics are the most troublesome of the waste stream, for many reasons. Although they make up about 7 percent of our waste—

most of that being packaging—they comprise as much as 30 percent by volume of waste going into landfills. The qualities that have made plastic so attractive a substitute for glass, metal, and cardboard—its lightness, strength, and durability—have made it a hazard for marine animals. Seabirds, sea turtles, seals, and other creatures are increasingly dying from eating small pieces of floating plastic and getting tangled in lost or discarded plastic fishlines and gear, six-pack plastic holders, and generic plastic junk thrown off oceangoing vessels. In fall 1988, the coordinator of a nationwide beach cleanup announced that plastics were an overwhelmingly greater problem on beaches than medical wastes. Volunteers collected hundreds of tons of plastic from 1,800 miles of shoreline in sixteen states and Puerto Rico.

The replacement of glass containers and paper-based packaging with plastic is accelerating, so that plastics are expected to comprise about 10 percent of the waste stream by the year 2000. Recycling of plastic lags behind the rest of the recycling industry, but it is being prodded and driven by ordinances throughout the country that encourage or require recyclable or biodegradable beverage containers.

Currently three types of plastics can be recycled. Approximately 20 percent of PET (polyethylene terephthalate) soft drink and bottled water containers are being recycled today and reused for a variety of nonfood uses: as manufactured carpet backing and fiberfill for items such as sleeping bags and ski jackets and as an ingredient in refrigerator insulation, automobile bumpers and furniture, fiberglass bathtubs, showerstalls, swimming pools, appliance handles and housing, floor tiles, paintbrushes, and kitchen scouring pads.

Another growing use for plastics is milk jugs made of HDPE (high-density polyethylene). These plastic jugs can be recycled into trash cans, flowerpots, piping, traffic cones, and "plastic lumber" in place of lumber for railroad ties, decking for boat piers and docks, and fencing. The industry, driven by the growing consumer resistance to polystyrene, is beginning to recycle polystyrene foam in cups, plates, fast-food carryout containers, and packaging. The material is cleaned and converted into pellets that can be combined with other plastic materials to create plastic lumber. These pellets can also be used to make building insulation and packing material.

Plastics recycling is complicated by the fact that many resins are

Fortune reports that only 0.2 percent of plastics are recycled versus 11 percent for all recyclables combined and 55 percent for aluminum cans. Even if the industry's programs succeed, the magazine quotes an Exxon Chemical executive, plastics recycling will increase to only 1 percent.

Spencer, Massachusetts initiated a profitable waste oil collection program in the town garage of the Highway Department, where a collection center was established. The waste oil is burned in the garage's oil furnace, which heats the equipment maintenance area. The savings in oil enabled the program to pay for itself in two years.

Massachusetts state law requires the store that sells a person motor oil to accept used oil free of charge with proof of purchase.

used in the manufacture of plastics and two lookalike bottles may be made of different resins. Thanks to new ordinances and public outcry, coding on bottles will begin to identify the resin type to aid in sorting for recycling. Commingling of various plastic types will probably increase, and the recycled mix will then be reused as a dense material in fence posts and park benches.

Recycling of plastic, however, does not solve the plastic waste issue as does recycling for glass and paper. Unlike glass and metal, plastic cannot yet be recycled back to its original uses—PET bottles back to PET bottles, for example—so that **recycling plastic does not reduce the manufacture of plastic nor the volume of plastic waste**. It will, in fact, create more and new uses for plastic as the recycled plastics industry finds new markets for its product. Recycling of plastic will only increase the amount of plastic in use while consumers are lulled into thinking that environmental concerns over plastics are being allayed. Recycling of plastic, currently at a rate of less than 1 percent of all plastics used, may thus obscure the growth in plastic use and dull concern over the geometric increase in unnecessary plastic packaging.

Motor Oil

Oil can be recycled in a process known as rerefining. Rerefining methods for lubricating oil were developed as early as 1915. Rerefined oil, however, is used mainly in industrial lubricating oils and gear-box oils. Although some of it is blended into automobile lubricating oils and sold as rerefined product, it has not made a major breakthrough in the large automobile market. Much used motor oil is processed and reused as fuel in incinerators.

EPA statistics show that only about 60 percent of all new motor oil sold can be accounted for later in the waste stream. One solution for recovering all waste oil is to provide a convenient collection place and then reuse the oil in municipal waste oil burners. Any town with a heated maintenance garage can offer this solution.

Scrap Tires

Over a billion scrap tires are stockpiled around the country. Landfilling is prohibited in many states because tires have a ten-

Cities pay about 10¢ per pound to dispose of old tires. A medium-sized city might pay about $700,000 a year to bury tires. A crumb rubber processing and manufacturing plant to recycle old tires could add up to $3 million to a local economy.

Minnesota banned tires from landfills. Using a special loan package, the state attracted a firm that processes old tires into crumb rubber to develop a plant. This plant was built in a low-income community, thereby providing jobs, and also attracted a crumb rubber end user to locate its plant nearby.

dency to rise to the surface in a landfill and crack the impervious landfill cap. Abandoned tires collect water and become a breeding ground for mosquitos. If ignited, they burn for months, creating air and groundwater contamination. Retreading tires requires about 30 percent of the energy necessary to produce new tires and provides nearly 80 percent of the mileage of a new tire. Almost 20 million truck tires and 17 million passenger tires are retreaded annually. Old tires can be recycled by grinding, shredding, and pulverizing the tires. The materials are then formed into sheet rubber and used to make molded materials and semipneumatic tires. Crumb rubber, or ground and shredded rubber, can be added to bituminous concrete to make asphalt rubber and used as an interlayer in pavement to reduce stress and prevent cracks in pavement. Rubber tires, a valuable material and potential energy source, have been a disposal problem because the markets for scrap tires are underdeveloped. Tire recycling is an infant industry with enormous potential.

Wood Waste/Yard Waste/Kitchen Waste

Wood waste, yard waste, and kitchen scraps comprise 18 to 25 percent of solid waste and offer an excellent opportunity for recycling. Many communities already compost this fraction of the waste stream, then use the compost in city parks, sell it to private landscape contractors, and make it available to residents. Some cities are encouraging residents to compost their own yard waste.

❏ ❏ ❏

Seattle encourages home composting in a comprehensive community composting education program. The program distributes an instructional brochure on how to compost yard and kitchen wastes and thus installed a composting hotline. People can tour a backyard composting demonstration site and train in a master composter program. A composting slide show and composting portable display are available for use in communities and schools.

❏ ❏ ❏

The crisis in solid waste is usually captured in repulsive profiles

DO YOU KNOW THAT . . .

Recycling the paper from one Sunday edition of the *New York Times* would save 75,000 trees.

The construction cost of a paper mill designed to use wastepaper is 50 percent to 80 percent less than the cost of a mill for new pulp.

Recycling plastics saves twice as much energy as burning them in an incinerator.

Recycling aluminum requires only 5 percent as much energy as producing it from bauxite. Each recycled beverage can saves the energy equivalent of half a can of gasoline.

Aluminum, nonrefillable glass, and steel can be recycled almost indefinitely.

SOURCE: R.W. Beck and Associates, "Recycling Implementation: Formula for Success," *Solid Waste Issues and Answers*, no. 2 (1989).

Food Business Magazine cited Campbell's "Souper Combo" as one of the five finest products of 1988. *Food and Drug Packaging Magazine* named it "Package of the Year." "Souper Combo" offers a sandwich and soup, 11.9 ounces of food wrapped in six layers of packaging, five of them plastic.

of skyscraperlike landfills and garbage-laden barges. The roots of the crisis lie, however, in something attractive and progressive looking: the use of packaging to sell products and to create consumer needs. The U.S. waste stream is glutted with consumer products and their packaging. Take food, for example: Between 1963 and 1971 the average person ate 2.3 percent more food, but food packaging rose 33 percent per person.

Between 1950 and 1986, the number of items carried by supermarkets increased five times, due to the phenomenal growth in the variety of hair coloring products, stomach relief products, and deodorants. Many products are priced somewhat comparably; advertising and packaging have replaced price competition to attract the consumer. The end result is that **packaging materials constitute the single largest component of municipal solid waste;** and the United States has the largest waste stream in the world. **Five percent of the world's people generate 40 percent of the world's waste.**

Only a few years ago, environmentalists and solid waste managers stood on different ends of the spectrum of solutions to the solid waste crisis. Public agencies and officials were reaching for state-of-the-art landfills and waste-to-energy incinerators as a first solution. Environmentalists were calling for comprehensive planning leading to *reduction, reuse, and recycling* of the waste stream. Only when the waste stream is shrunken to its minimum flow should we plan for disposal of the remaining waste by incineration, landfill, or alternative, innovative waste technologies.

Today, there is a near national consensus on solid waste: **Reduce, reuse and recycle first; then, and only then, dispose**. The consensus is driven by a few engines: One is public outrage against new landfills and incinerators, so that public agencies have to forestall the crisis of running out of landfill space by starting aggressive recycling programs in their communities. Another is a rapidly rising demand for less packaging where possible along with recyclable and biodegradable containers and packaging. This demand is fast being addressed by thousands of pieces of legislation. In 1987, *Packaging* magazine conducted a consumer survey on packaging. In response to the question, "How often does the recyclability of a package affect your decision to buy one product over another," 41 percent of respondents said "often" or "sometimes." This was an increase of 5 percent from 1986. A 1989 survey by the Michael Peters Group, a New York- and London-based consulting firm, found that 78 percent of 1000 Americans surveyed were willing to pay up to five percent more for a product packaged in recyclable or biodegradable materials.

Reducing, reusing, and recycling our waste—in that order—is state-of-the-art policy in solid waste management. Let us look at a blueprint for reaching that goal.

RESOURCES

Reading/Information

Designing the Waste Stream (1988)
Neil Seldman and Bill Perkins
Institute for Local Self-Reliance
2425 18th Street NW

Washington, DC 20009
(202) 232-4108
$12

Also from the Institute for Local Self-Reliance: *Proven Profits from Pollution Prevention: Case Studies in Resource Conservation and Waste Reduction* (1986)
$25

Proven Profits from Pollution Prevention, vol. 2 (1989)
$20

Resource Recycling
P.O. Box 10540
Portland, Oregon 97210
(503) 227-1319

Published monthly by Resource Recycling, Inc., an organization not affiliated with a trade association. Provides analytical news in the recycling field.

Chapter 5

The Three Rs
of Solid Waste:
Reduce, Reuse, Recycle

Patricia Poore, the editor of *Old House Journal*, recently started a national how-to environmental magazine for city and suburban dwellers that she named *Garbage*. The inspiration goes back to the 1960s when Poore spent a year in India, where she saw food and materials recycled and reused so thoroughly that there was "no such thing as garbage." But why this name for her magazine? Because, she editorializes, garbage is waste, and waste is at the core of pollution: "wasteful habits, solid waste, waste of resources, hazardous waste, waste that pollutes and enters the food chain."

If waste is the core of pollution, then conservation is the heart of living as if the Earth mattered. Conservation means, simply, decreasing the amount of waste we create and getting off the "consume it/trash it treadmill," as Poore puts it. The blueprint for radically reducing the amount of your garbage and minimizing its harm to the environment is: **Shop selectively; reuse and recycle; and compost**.

❑ ❑ ❑

Selective shopping to avoid plastics and reduce paper use can remove 10 to 20 percent from the household garbage cans.

❑ ❑ ❑

WHAT YOU CAN DO

1. Shop Selectively.

My neighbors, friends, and colleagues at work welcomed the chance to offer concrete examples of environmentally conscious shopping. Here is their advice—simple, sensible, and decidedly "one person's impact."

Buy durable rather than disposable products—for example, ceramic mugs, razors with replaceable blades. Buy in bulk quantity bagged from bulk bins; buy large boxes of laundry detergent to minimize packaging waste along with concentrates that can be diluted for use. Buy sensibly packaged products, ones that use less rather than more packaging. Buy products that are packaged in recyclable or recycled materials—beverages in glass or aluminum containers, takeout foods packaged in paper rather than plastic foam. Reuse plastic produce bags. Bring a cloth bag when going shopping.

The Regional Solid Waste Disposal Project of Spokane, Washington has developed a shopping checklist (shown on page 59) to help consumers develop buying habits that show respect for the environment.

Disposable Diapers

A baby sits with a pile of forty cotton diapers on her left, which can be washed and reused, and 10,000 plastic disposable diapers on her right, looking like the high-rise landfill they will soon be thrown into. This image sums up the voluminous, unnecessary waste generated in the United States. The wide difference in waste between reusable cotton diapers and plastic throwaway ones parallels the diaper industry fortunes. The diaper service industry once had 700 companies; now it has 100. Disposable diaper sales soared from $90 million in 1969 to $3.3 billion in 1987. As for advertising, disposable diaper ads are using the same packaging gimmicks to sell their product that cosmetic and health products use: colored diapers, Sesame Street diapers, and so on.

SHOPPING CHECKLIST

1.□ Do I need this product?

2.□ Is the package recyclable or returnable?

3.□ Does a similar product come with less packaging?

4.□ Can I re-use this disposable product?

5.□ Is there a non-disposable alternative?

6.□ How many times can I use this product before I throw it away?

7.□ How long will this product last?

8.□ Can this product be repaired rather than discarded?

9.□ If the product is something I seldom use can I borrow or rent it?

10.□ Will the disposal of this product be a hazard to the environment? If so, is there a safer alternative?

Disposable diapers make a convenient symbol of our throwaway society and our garbage crisis. They cost more than their reusable alternative (22¢ vs 15¢); the plastic liners last "forever" in a landfill; they are contaminated with fecal waste that carries bacteria and viruses. But, we may ask, is it accurate or fair to lay the blame on those who do child care in our society?

Is It Accurate?

The environmental problems of disposable diapers can be mitigated with some effort. Diapers should be emptied into the toilet before they are thrown away in order to put feces into the sewage system and keep it out of landfills. But one study cited by the *New York Times* reports that fewer than 5 percent of people who care for children take this sanitary measure. Biodegradable diapers that contain cornstarch are appearing on the market. *Seventh Generation* catalogue, which sells them, states that they are as comfortable and absorbent as regular diapers and that they degrade within two to five years in landfills. My own informal survey of users, however, revealed that biodegradable diapers do not perform as well as the best absorbent ones. And environmental critics of biodegradable plastic warn that nothing degrades predictably in landfills in two to five years.

Is It Fair?

Unlike many other alleged labor-saving inventions for child and home care, disposable diapers have substantially eased one aspect of child care. Ask the people who do it, women. And diapers constitute only about 2 percent of the entire solid waste stream, less than unnecessary plastic packaging. Until child care is equally shared by men and women—and all the recent surveys reveal that men do not share child care and housework equally with women, even though women make up nearly half the labor force—then environmentalists should target another component of the waste stream to symbolize the problem of waste.

Manufacturers need to make high-quality biodegradable diapers that compete with the best nonbiodegradable ones. Government should give diaper delivery services the same tax incentives that recycling operations receive in some states. Men should perform their fair share of diaper care. Then let's spotlight disposable diapers.

2. Recycle and Reuse.

Recycle through all the opportunities available. Besides curbside collection and dropoff sites, consider reselling goods by yard sales, consignment, or classified ads. Buy used and rebuilt goods, where possible; and donate toys, books, clothing, furniture, and utensils to nonprofit charitable organizations. Some recycling centers take used motor oil for free; some service stations recycle it for a small fee. Never put it in the garbage, down a storm drain, or into the ground.

Many states are adopting some form of recycling and reduction laws primarily to reduce the amount of waste going to landfills. In some cases, recycling is mandatory, with a penalty for noncompliance; in others, it is voluntary. Some cities, like Seattle, use a garbage fee system that provides financial incentives for recycling as much as possible. Here are some examples of the most comprehensive state legislation to mandate recycling.

New Jersey: Separation and Recycling by County

Resource Reclamation Inc. (ReClaim) is a remanufacturing facility in Kearny, New Jersey that recycles asphalt roofing scrap into a reusable road product. The roofing scrap is mechanically chopped into small pieces that measure one-half inch or less in width. The product is reused as a low-cost paving material for parking areas and equipment yards; as a pothole patching material; and as a low-cost amendment to hot asphalt mix. The fee for delivering a container of scrap to the facility is 50 percent of disposal costs at a landfill.

The 1987 Mandatory Statewide Source Separation and Recycling Act requires that residents separate leaves and at least three marketable materials such as newspaper, glass, and cans. Each county develops its own plan, designates a recycling coordinator, and specifies marketing strategies for recycled materials. Municipalities can impose fines or refuse garbage service to offenders. The state assists with developing recycling and composting markets and earmarks the revenue from a surcharge on waste disposal for a statewide recycling fund. In support of recycling market development, the 1987 act commits the state to purchase products made from recycled materials. Leaf compost material, for example, is given priority for use on state lands. The Department of Transportation has altered its bid specifications for highway materials to encourage the use of crumb rubber, a material recycled from used tires.

Florida: A Sweeping New Policy

The June 1988 Solid Waste Management Bill is one of the boldest examples of mandatory state recycling legislation. The bill establishes a 30 percent reduction/recycling goal by 1994 in a state where recycling programs were virtually nonexistent and pilot projects had less than 5 percent participation rate. Materials that must be separated and recycled are newspaper, glass, plastic bottles, metal cans, lead-acid batteries, tires, used oil, and yard waste. In addition, the bill sets deadlines by which packaging containing chlorofluorocarbons (chemicals that deplete the ozone layer) is prohibited and plastic bags for consumer products, plastic rings on beverages, and polystyrene foam packaging must be biodegradable (time frames set on biodegradability). By July 1, 1992, plastic containers must be labeled with the type of resin used in the bottle to facilitate recycling. With a mix of sales taxes, business registration fees, oil overcharge settlement funds, and disposal fees, the state created a trust fund to aid local governments. In addition, Florida has mandated waste reduction and recycling by all state agencies and the use of recycled and recovered materials where feasible in construction, highway, and parks projects. The Department of Education must develop guidelines for school recycling programs and curriculum materials for recycling for all school grade levels.

Washington: Top Priority to Reduction and Recycling

The state's 1989 recycling bill sets a goal of 50 percent waste reduction and recycling by 1995. The bill sets waste reduction and recycling as the preferred and first method of statewide waste handling. Beginning October 1, 1989, a $1 fee will be placed on the retail sale of new tires for five years. The seller will retain 10 percent of the fee to pay for handling waste tires. Ninety percent of the fee will be deposited in a state fund that will finance pilot projects for on-site shredding and recycling of tires from unauthorized dump sites. Stores that sell automotive batteries must accept their customers' used ones. Customers who don't return a used battery when purchasing a new one must pay a $5 fee. State government buildings will purchase recycled products and implement recycling and hazardous waste reduction programs. A 1 percent state tax will be levied on garbage bills through June 1993 to generate funds for research on hard-to-recycle materials, to help develop markets for recycled products, and to assist local government programs.

Recycling paper, metal, and glass can eliminate 20 to 40 percent of the household garbage.

The New Statutes and Kitchen Design

The biggest concern that mandatory recycling creates in the household is the prospect of clutter when separate containers are needed for cans, paper, plastic, and compostable garbage. Because most kitchens are small and already crowded, people resort to storing recycling bins in closets, hallways, cellars, garages, porches, and yards. One dedicated recycler tells of taking over her one-car garage for bins and parking her car outside! Kitchen and home designers are devising all kinds of interesting waste storage areas, some adapted from the concepts of built-in food storage containers of early kitchens, dumb waiters, and laundry chutes. My favorite is a "recycling island" with tilt-out bins for cans, paper, plastic, reusable plastic containers, and compost waste. Above the compost bin, a hole is cut into the food preparation countertop for easy disposal of nonmeat food scraps.

3. Compost.

Composting turns wastes like grass clippings, leaves, weeds, the remains of garden plants, and nonmeat kitchen wastes into a dark, fresh-smelling organic material that resembles soil humus. Putting compost in your garden, you return organic matter to its source, soil, in a form that is beneficial to plants. Compost improves the water-holding properties of soil, helps it to stay aerated, and adds back essential nutrients for growing plants.

The key ingredients of a compost heap include a container, biodegradable wastes, moisture, aeration, and microorganisms. Compost piles are typically framed by wood, wire, or concrete blocks, although leaves can be composted in heaps 4 to 10 feet in diameter and 3 to 5 feet high. The ideal size for your backyard compost pile is a 3-foot cube, large enough to insulate itself and hold the heat of microbial activity, small enough to allow air to reach the microbial organisms at the center. Compost teems with millions of microorganisms feeding on and decomposing your kitchen and yard wastes. Bacteria start the process of decomposition and are later joined by fungi and protozoans. Centipedes, millipedes, beetles, and earthworms finish transforming yard and kitchen waste to beneficial organic material. Carbon and nitrogen in dead plants, sawdust, and kitchen nonmeat waste provide food and energy for the explosion of microbial life in the compost pile. The ideal ratio of carbon to nitrogen for compost life is 30:1, achieved by two parts leaves to one part grass clippings, or other comparable sources of carbon and nitrogen. The smaller the pieces the waste is chopped or cut into, the faster the microorganisms will decompose them. Microbes function best when the compost materials are about as moist as a wrung-out sponge and well aerated.

Composting is like cooking and gardening—there are as many ways to do it as there are aficionados (see the Resources section).

❑ ❑ ❑

My mother buries her nonmeat kitchen scraps in 8-inch deep holes in her backyard vegetable garden, enough of a distance from her plants not to injure their roots. She reports that small, once-thin garden worms are now plump and long.

I constructed simple, lightweight, portable compost containers from flexible wire fencing. They are 3 feet in diameter and stand 3 feet high. To aerate the heap, I lift off the wire frame, place it next to the original pile, and shovel the composting material back into it. Recently I discovered a low-tech tool for aerating the pile that saves the labor of removing the frame and turning the composting material back into it. The aerator is a 32-inch-high piece of pipe with a two-hand grip handle on top and and twin movable metal pieces at the bottom end. I insert it deep into the compost pile, turn it a few times, and pull it back up. With my turning and pulling up, the two movable parts catch and pull material on the bottom to the top of the pile, material at the side to the center, aerating and mixing the waste for even composting. I don't generally have ideal proportions of grass to leaves, or other carbon to nitrogen sources. Rather, my compost waste is seasonal: ten parts leaves to one part grass during the fall; kitchen waste and wood ash all winter; raked grass in spring; garden plants and cut grass in summer; and often some soil. So my compost heap takes longer—10 months—to break down into moist, dark, earthy-smelling organic material than the fast, hot, efficient ones built of thirty parts carbon and one part nitrogen.

❑ ❑ ❑

Many waste managers have admitted that if they could start their recycling programs over, they would target yard waste sooner rather than later. Composting yard waste, which now makes up an average of 18 percent of the waste stream, can reduce landfill burdens more than any other waste material except mixed paper.

Composting of yard and food waste can eliminate 15 to 20 percent of household garbage.

❏ ❏ ❏

The state of Maine offered grants to attract proposals for beneficial reuse of fish wastes—bones, guts, heads, and tails—from fish processing companies. One company is turning the wastes into compost, an idea taught to Pilgrims by native Americans who placed fish remains in holes together with corn seeds. Another firm is turning the fish waste into feed for animals and fish. A unique third development is a liquid spray that, when sprayed on Maine potato fields, appears to kill weeds, repress bacterial diseases, provide nutrients, and ward off the Colorado potato beetle. How beneficial could this reuse of fish waste in agriculture prove to be? Aroostook County, Maine, an area as large as the state of Massachusetts, is the third largest regional producer of potatoes after Idaho and Washington state. In Maine, twenty-eight different agricultural chemicals—fertilizers, and pesticides—are used to grow potatoes. A half dozen insecticides, herbicides, and nitrates from fertilizer have been detected in groundwater.

❏ ❏ ❏

WHAT YOU CAN DO: At Work

The average office employee generates 1.2 pounds of waste paper per day. High-quality paper makes up 40 percent of this material. Corrugated cardboard represents about half the waste in retail stores and warehouses. What can be done to reduce this figure?

1. Recycle.

Recycle as much office waste as possible: mail, office paper, computer paper, newsprint, corrugated cardboard, aluminum cans, some plastic, litho film, X-ray film, printing film, glass bottles and jars, wiring, lead, aluminum, iron, copper, brass.

2. Reduce and Reuse.

Reduce the amount of copies by circulating memos. Use electronic mail instead of paper. Make two-sided copies whenever possible. Maintain a central filing system. Choose durable reusable items instead of disposable ones—coffee mugs, for example, instead of styrofoam cups. Use returnable or reusable containers for storage and shipping. Donate old furniture and other office equipment to local charitable organizations. Find the regional materials exchange center that facilitates the exchange of materials and information.

3. Buy Recycled.

Does your company or workplace have a recycling program? Do they have a "buy recycled" policy? If your company has a newsletter, use this medium as a way to raise the issue and create awareness and interest in it.

"If you're not buying recycled products, you're not recycling"— this is the motto one company uses. Waste Management, Inc., which recycles the garbage of more than 600,000 households in the United States and Canada, has a company-wide policy of buying recycled products. The company uses recycled paper and has a goal of using 100 percent recycled stationery. They are looking next to building and construction products that contain or are derived from recycled products for their building projects, which include offices, maintenance buildings, and recycling/transfer stations. They are exploring the use of recycled plastics in their solid waste and recycling containers. Waste Management has been retreading tires for their large vehicles for years. They also retread the casings as long as the casings are sound.

WHAT YOU CAN DO: In the Schools

Does your community school have a recycling program and curriculum? If not, talk to the principal or someone in the science department about starting one.

Every successful municipal recycling program has stressed the importance of engaging community schools in recycling and offering a curriculum in recycling. Calling it *recycling literacy*, Neil Seldman of the Institute for Local Self-Reliance says that in-school education is far more effective and lasting than general public awareness. "Like reading and writing, once recycling is taught, it is never forgotten." And students who learn to recycle in school bring home the awareness and the habit.

❏ ❏ ❏

During the past decade recycling projects at Wesleyan University have primarily been products of student initiative. Although successful, these efforts were often short lived because students who developed them graduated. Connecticut recently passed mandatory recycling laws. This ensures that the recycling program at Wesleyan, for which students have been hired as planners and developers together with University staff, will endure. The plan is aimed at three types of paper flow: computer, high grade/confidential office paper, and mixed paper (ledger, colored, newspaper, and magazines). The projected first-year costs for the program, which include bin rental, publicity, physical plant, and student labor, are $13,742. The projected first-year savings in avoided tipping fees at landfills is $27,635.

❏ ❏ ❏

Solid waste is the pollution issue in which the connection between our actions and their effect on the environment is most direct and immediate. An aluminum can I recycle does not get buried in a landfill; 95 percent of the energy needed to make a new can is conserved. Using a ceramic coffee mug in the office instead of a disposable polystyrene cup eliminates voluminous plastic waste, saves on petrochemicals used in manufacturing, and protects the ozone layer.

To inspire personal action, Sarah Blair and Maria Valenti founded and edit *One Person's Impact*, a bimonthly newsletter featuring practical, small-scale suggestions for recycling, ridding your house and neighborhood of toxic hazards, and making a difference through selective buying. Valenti explains that she could not put down a story on global warming or depletion of the ozone layer without trying to figure out what she herself could do about it. She came to believe one person can make a difference when a legislator she had been lobbying signed a proposed environmental bill because of her influence. Both editors have tried all the solutions they recommend, such as salt and cayenne pepper for pest control; and lemon juice, vinegar, and baking soda for household cleansers. They recycle and review recycling centers; they nominate local retailers who use or sell environmentally sensitive products. Their newsletter is printed on recycled paper. "You may find, as we have," they write, "that as you adopt certain ecologically sensitive habits, subtle changes occur in your philosophy of life" (see the Resources section).

One change, for many of us, has been to minimize the use of plastic. Plastic was once decried as a blight that lasts forever. Now some plastic is "degradable." Plastic is blamed for taking up more space in landfills per unit than any other waste because it is bulky, even when lightweight. Now some plastic is recyclable. Recently, two writers summed up the complexities of this most dominant of synthetics in the title of their feature article, "The Power of Plastic: The Good, the Bad, and the Ugly." The decision to use or not use plastic—a biodegradable plastic shopping bag versus a brown paper bag; a recyclable plastic beverage container versus glass—is not as clearcut as it was before plastic was degradable and recyclable. Let's look more closely at these options.

RESOURCES

Guides to Action/Organizations

Buy Recycled

Resource Recycling
P.O. Box 10540
Portland, OR 97210
(503) 227-1319

Recommend any office buying recycled products to contact *Resource Recycling* for list of products, catalogues, companies, services, etc.

Earth Care Paper Company
P.O. Box 3335
Madison, WI 53704
(608) 256-5522

Recycled paper products for home and office.

Composting

Community Composting Education Program
"Home Composting"

710 2nd Avenue, Suite 750
Seattle, WA 98410
Free

Rodale Guide to Composting (1979)
Rodale Books
33 East Minor St.
Emmaus, PA 18098
$14.95

Kitchen Design

The Smart Kitchen: How to Design a Comfortable, Safe, Energy-Efficient, and Money-Saving Workplace (1989)
David Goldbeck
Ceres Press
Dept. GM, PO Box 87
Woodstock, NY 12498
$17.95

Organizing a Community Program

Coming Full Circle, Successful Recycling Today (1988)
Environmental Defense Fund
257 Park Avenue South
New York, NY 10010
(212) 505-2100
$20

Recycling reference including information on successful recycling programs, local planning, and developing markets for recyclable materials.

Ten Steps to Organizing a Community Recycling Program
Pennsylvania Roadside Council
44 East Front St.
Media, PA 19063
(215) 565-9131

Resources

Garbage
P.O. Box 56520
Boulder, CO 80321-6520
Bimonthly, $21/year

One Person's Impact
P.O. Box 751
Westborough, MA 01581
Sarah Blair (508) 478-3716
Maria Valenti (508) 366-0146
Bimonthly, $24/year

Selective Shopping

Become an Environmental Shopper (1988)
Pennsylvania Roadside Council
44 East Front St.
Media, PA 19063
(215) 565-9131
$5

Seventh Generation
Catalogue of Products for a Healthy Planet
10 Farrell St.
South Burlington, VT 05403
(802) 862-2999
$2

Shopping for a Better World
Council on Economic Priorities
30 Irving Place
New York, New York 10003
800-U-CAN-HELP
$5.95

Booklet rates 1,300 household products based on their manufacturers'
performance in areas like affirmative action, animal testing, and the
environment. Condensed into a 22-item hot sheet for use in the supermarket:
"The List."
$5

Chapter 6

Plastics: Bane or Boon?

If brewers were forbidden to put plastic nooses on six-packs of beer, if supermarkets were not allowed to wrap polyvinyl chloride film around everything in sight, if McDonalds restaurants could rediscover the paper plate, if the use of plastics were cut back to those things considered worth the social costs . . . then we could push back the petrochemical industry's toxic invasion of the biosphere.

Barry Commoner, in *Greenpeace* magazine (1989)

"**I**n our every deliberation, we must consider the impact of our decisions on the next seven generations," declared the Six Nations Iroquois Confederacy—a consideration never given to the production and proliferation of plastic. I walked through my neighborhood and filled a shopping bag full of plastic litter caught in bushes, thrown in ditches, and blown from garbage trucks on collection day. A potpourri of soda bottles, coffee cups, an empty motor oil container, candy wrappers, individual fruit juice containers, potato chip bags, styrofoam packing pellets, and plastic strapping from crates—none degradable. Had I not collected them, they would still be there, or wherever else they were carried by wind and rain, through "seven generations."

Now that I own this bag of plastic litter, it will be put out with my nonrecyclable trash, which gets dumped in the town landfill. There it will remain intact for dozens, if not hundreds, of years. Plastic is no better disposed in a landfill than on roadsides, since it doesn't go away in either place. This fact illustrates one problem with plastics—it is litter that lasts. And lots of it lasts, because only a small fraction of plastic is degradable.

But what if this bag of plastic litter were degradable—a recent development that is often touted as solving the problem of plastics' immortality? (Europe has been using degradable plastic for some twenty years now. Italy has mandated that all film in plastic packaging be degradable by 1990.) Degradable plastic is either broken down into small pieces by bacteria in soil, in which case it is "biodegradable," or by the ultraviolet rays of the sun on it, in which case it is "photodegradable." Plastics are made of polymers or long chains of homogeneous hydrocarbon molecules that are so tightly bound together that microscopic fungi and bacteria that dissolve leaves, wood, and other organic material cannot penetrate them. This accounts for the strength and durability of plastic.

Biodegradable plastic has some additional cellulose or starches, such as corn or rice starch, that can be eaten by soil bacteria. Once this process starts, the rest of the plastic material becomes susceptible to breakdown by microorganisms. The period of time required for substantial degradation depends on the amount of starch added to the resin, the composition of the soil, and the amount of heat and moisture. Some scientists are working with bacteria that manufacture a natural polymer that has the strength of plastic but is naturally biodegradable by microbes.

Photodegradables are made by adding light-sensitive chemicals to polymer chains. When they are exposed to ultraviolet rays of sunlight, the chemicals make the polymer chains weaken and break down into smaller units. The plastic becomes brittle and disintegrates into smaller and smaller pieces.

Neither type of degradable plastic eliminates the mounting trash in landfills, since any waste buried breaks down very slowly and photodegradable plastic has no access to sunlight. Photodegradable plastic floating on the sea is still sufficiently long lived to entrap and harm marine life. There are other serious issues outstanding for degradable plastics. Do degradables really degrade as well as claimed? Little testing has been done to prove the claim of degradability. Are the residues—small pieces of plastics and chemical additives—safe as residues in the environment? Will the proliferation of degradable plastics frustrate the recycling of plastics, and thwart the more important effort of reducing the proliferation in plastic, if the consumer thinks that the problem of plastic is solved when it is degradable? **Are degradable plastics good for the environment?**

Using degradable plastic makes people feel good by creating the impression that degradable plastic is an environmental boon. Jeanne Wirka of Environment Action calls degradable plastic "a consumer rip-off." Degradable plastic, if mixed with recyclable plastic, will contaminate the recycling process. Degradable plastic encourages the use of plastic and does not stem the growth of plastic packaging.

A rapid review of the history of plastics shows the phenomenal growth in plastic material and waste over the past fifty years and conveys the industry's plans for future growth.

GROWTH OF PLASTICS

The first commercial plastic, celluloid, was developed in 1869 by an entrepreneurial maker of dental plates and novelty items. He answered an ad placed by a supplier of billiards equipment offering a reward for developing a suitable replacement material for elephant ivory to make billiard balls. In 1889, Eastman Kodak began to use celluloid in photographic film. The only surviving commercial use of celluloid is in the manufacture of ping-pong balls. In the early 1900s, a chemist-inventor was attempting to make a substitute for shellac and produced a material that was patented as Bakelite.

The real commercial development of plastics began during World War II for mass production of such objects as plastic bugles, canteens, and dinnerware—and has skyrocketed since. In the past fifty years, plastics production has increased from virtually nothing to 50 billion pounds per year—about 10 pounds for every person in the world! The growth in plastics can be marked by American cultural milestones, as Figure 6.1 shows.

In 1939, nylon stockings were introduced at the World's Fair. A year later, polyvinylidene chloride, named Saran, was invented; by 1955, more than 5 million rolls of Saran Wrap were sold each month. In 1957, Monsanto built a "House of the Future," with walls, roof, floors, rugs, and furniture of plastic—at the entrance of Tomorrowland at Disneyland. A decade later wrecking balls could not demolish it—neither could blowtorches, chainsaws, and jackhammers. Cables had to be attached to tear the house apart. That same year, the polyethylene hula hoop was invented, and millions of children who played with hula hoops would grow up with plastic as common a material in their lives as glass and metal.

In the 1970s and 1980s, microwave ovens and microwave cook-

Figure 6.1 Growth of Plastics Production in the United States

Adapted from: *A Citizen's Guide to Plastics in the Ocean* (Washington, D.C., 1988).

1939 World War II speeds plastics development with plastic bugles, canteens, and navy dinnerware among the multitude of uses.

1939 Nylon stockings debut at the World's Fair, later to create stocking riots of the 1940s.

1940 Polyvinylidene chloride is named Saran—first used to make suspenders.

1940 The Christmas tree in Rockefeller Center is lighted with specially designed plastic ornaments, replacing glass ornaments from Europe.

1946 Earl S. Tupper produces a 7-ounce polyethylene tumbler, the first of many items later available from Tupperware Home Parties Inc; nylon zippers and acrylic dentures are introduced.

1950s Plastics expand in packaging applications.

1955 The Corvette is the first car to use plastic for body panels.

1957 Monsanto's House of Tomorrow opens in Disneyland with walls, roof, floors, rugs, and furniture made of plastic.

1957 Invention of hula hoop creates surge in demand for polyethylene.

1964 Michelangelo's *Pieta* cushioned in plastics for shipment from Vatican to the 1964 New York World's Fair.

1967 "I just want to say one word to you...plastics"—business advice to Dustin Hoffman's character in *The Graduate*.

1969 Man and plastics land on the moon.

1976 Plastic microwave cookware available to consumers.

1979 "T-Shirt" style plastic grocery bags test marketing proves to be successful.

1982 Dr. Robert Jarvik designs the artificial heart made largely of plastics.

1983 Microwave ovens open a new market for plastic packaging.

1986 The flight of the *Voyager* demonstrates the capabilities of advanced plastics composites when the 2,600-pound aircraft (including pilots) successfully flies around the world without refueling.

ware, Gor-Tex sportswear, Teflon, increasing use of plastic in cars, home appliances, medical technology, packaging, and now plastic 2 x 4's show that the markets for plastic are "plastic" indeed. The General Electric Company recently introduced a prototype two-story, "single-family" plastic house in Pittsfield, Massachusetts, with walls, ceilings, roof, windows and structural elements mostly plastic. GE predicts that engineered plastics, which will be recycled from other waste plastics such as plastic packaging and containers, will gradually replace other building materials because of their superior endurance. They do not crack, peel, warp, or absorb moisture. (What happens in the event of fire?)

It is estimated that by the end of the century, 28,000 firms—30 percent more than today—will be operating in one or more branches of the plastics industry. The use of plastics in the food industry is projected to double, reaching fully 40 percent of packaging materials; plastic shopping bags, holding 25 percent of the market, will grow to 75 percent.

Many analysts recognize that the chemical industry has turned to degradable plastics out of fear that packagers will return to paper, aluminum, or glass if restrictions on plastic use and popular opinion against plastics both increase. Degradable plastic shopping bags are being marketed as "environmentally safe." But are they? The chemical industries that make the resins and polymers and the processors who turn them into degradable and nondegradable plastic bags generate billions of pounds of hazardous waste per year. Additives such as colorants, plasticizers, and stabilizers can be toxic constituents that remain in the soil when biodegradable plastic breaks down or that pollute the air when the plastic waste is incinerated.

❏ ❏ ❏

The Franklin County, Massachusetts Trash Education Project organized Environmental Shoppers Week. Members of the project organized a petition for local markets to reduce packaging and plastic. They distributed flyers to markets and shoppers with a list of recommendations: use recycled paper bags rather than plastic bags at the cash register and for produce, glass bottles instead of plastic containers for liquids, and paper and cardboard instead of styrofoam and plastic for packaging meats.

❏ ❏ ❏

WHAT YOU CAN DO

---

1. Don't use plastic shopping bags. Choose recyclable paper bags. Bring your own cloth bag.

2. Organize a petition to request that area supermarkets reduce their use of packaging and plastic.

3. Choose recyclable glass and metal containers rather than recyclable or degradable plastic ones.

The most immediate problem that increasing plastic creates is in disposal. Although plastic represents a small percent of the municipal garbage (about 7%), plastic is bulky, taking up an average of 30 percent of the garbage volume. The days of simply using and throwing away plastic are numbered, as landfills close and no new ones reopen. In some places—neighborhoods and city streets—plastics debris is unsightly and ugly. When it is disposed of, the same debris rapidly fills up landfills squeezed for space. In the sea and marine environments, plastics debris is "more than a litter problem," as the Center for Marine Conservation puts it—it is dangerous.

PLASTICS IN THE MARINE ENVIRONMENT ———————

Plastics are the most common human-made objects seen at sea: One survey of the North Pacific Ocean found that 86 percent of floating trash was plastic. Plastic is lightweight, making it preferable to heavier materials for use in packaging. But plastic is also buoyant. At least fifty of the world's 280 species of seabirds eat small pieces of floating plastic that resemble plankton or fish eggs that also float. Five species of sea turtles confuse floating plastic bags and wrap for their prey, jellyfish. These marine animals may eventually die from malnutrition and other complications. Green sea turtles died en masse off the coast of Costa Rica from ingesting plastic banana bags thrown overboard.

Degradable plastic does not solve the hazard of plastic to marine animals. Marine debris is still marine debris, and dangerous for sea mammals, even if its life span is shortened in degradable plastic. For this reason, Maine has banned plastic six-pack rings on beverages, whether or not they are photodegradable.

Plastic is strong and durable; it does not rot, decay, tear, crack, or dissolve when thrown away or lost at sea. Before World War II, fishing nets were made of natural fibers that sank to the ocean floor and disintegrated when they were lost or discarded. Larger, lightweight, durable plastic nets have replaced those nets. Once they are discarded or lost, they can float for years as "ghost nets" catching, trapping, and killing unwary birds and marine animals. Fifty thousand Northern Fur seals drown each year in the North Pacific because they are trapped in more than 600 miles of fish netting that is lost or discarded at sea annually, mainly by Japanese fishing vessels.

Plastic is increasingly used on ships: for strapping in place of rope and steel; as shipping sacks and packaging materials. Every day, ships—merchant, commercial, navy, passenger, and recreational—throw 450,000 plastic containers into the world's seas. Each year fishermen dump more than 52 million pounds of plastic packaging material and 300 million pounds of plastic fishing gear into the sea. Trash from petroleum industry oil rigs and drilling platforms washes up onto local beaches. Plastic pellets, a raw form of plastic, are transported in bulk to manufacturing sites, where they are melted down and made into plastic consumer goods. Discarded and blown by the wind, these waste scraps from the melting process float on the sea, where they are ingested by seabirds. Plastics flushed into sewage systems—diapers, condoms, and tampon applicators—are often discharged directly into the sea.

Since 1975, plastic packaging has more than doubled. It is estimated that at present 20 percent of all packaging is plastic, but that by the year 2000 this figure will increase to 40 percent—metal cans and glass containers being the major targets to replace. With the increased use of plastic will come an increase in plastic pollution of the sea, which is not solved by degradable plastic.

WHAT YOU CAN DO

1. Organize a beach cleanup at your beach.

Ask the steering committee of the beach club, the local conservation commission, and the state Department of Natural Resources to help with the organiztion. Use the action to educate about beach waste and the hazards of plastic debris to marine life.

In November 1987, the United States ratified Annex V of the Marpol Convention, an international agreement that regulates pollution from ships. Annex V outlaws dumping of plastics at sea as of January 1, 1989. The Coast Guard is developing regulations to implement this requirement.

Newport, Oregon, a two-berth deepwater port with a 600-ship marina and 800 fishing vessels, has initiated a model pilot recycling program to discourage dumping waste at sea. Called the Marine Refuse Disposal Project, it combines enforcement of Annex V with recycling. Fishermen deposit plastic net and refuse, as well as metal and cardboard, into containers set up at the port. The net is reused by people in the community. Fishermen who were once the biggest skeptics now articulate the elements of success in this program: education and involving people. An advisory committee of commercial fishermen was formed at the planning stage; a fisherman artist developed the logo.

❏ ❏ ❏

Judie Nielson of the Oregon Department of Natural Resources translated her concern about plastic debris in the marine environment into action. She organized a cleanup of Oregon's 350 miles of coast with volunteers on an October Saturday morning in 1984. More than 2,000 people participated, some driving from 75 miles inland. They collected more than 26 tons of plastic debris, including polystyrene chunks, pieces of rope, plastic food utensils, bags or sheets of plastic, plastic bottles and strapping bands, six-pack rings, and fishing gear. Nielson's project inspired beach cleanups in all U.S. states and throughout the Mediterranean, in Egypt, France, Greece, Israel, Jordan, Morocco, Spain, and Turkey.

❏ ❏ ❏

2. Write to your Port Authority.

Write c/o the director and the chief of environmental management, and inquire what waste disposal facilities they offer to incoming commercial ships to discourage disposal at sea. If you use a marina, help organize an educational campaign for fishermen and recreational boaters around waste dumping at sea. Encourage your marina to provide waste disposal facilities for solid waste from boats.

RECYCLING

Recycling of plastics is an infant enterprise: Less than 1 percent of plastics were recycled in 1989, compared to 33 percent of aluminum and 21 percent of paper. Plastics are the easiest and cheapest material to recycle: Just shred, remelt usually at low temperatures, and reform in molds. The problems posed by recycling plastics, however, are twofold: separation (as we separate high-grade from mixed paper, clear from colored glass) and purification.

Two plastic bottles can look alike but be made of different plastic resins. Therefore, consumers can't identify and separate out plastics made of the same resin unless manufacturers mark the resin name on the plastic. Over the next few years, plastic bottlers will set up a voluntary coding system to identify resin types on 8-ounce and larger containers. That effort still excludes a large amount of postconsumer plastic. On the other hand, polyethylene terephthalate (PET) soda bottles and high-density polyethylene (HDPE) milk jugs are recognizable and can be separated out for recycling. They are not, however, recycled back into bottle containers like metal and glass because the plastic cannot be adequately purified in the recycling process for reuse in the food industry.

The result of this twofold dilemma in plastic recycling is that recycled plastics are not returned to their original use. Recycled bottles are made into carpet fibers, cushion stuffing, and scouring pads. Mixed plastics are made into lumberlike poles, post stakes, and slats for building never-rotting barns, docks, fences, road markers, and pilings. These latter developments will save on the use of wood and last much longer than a wood counterpart. But this kind of recycling does not challenge the enormous growth in unnecessary plastic packaging. Because the material is marked "recyclable," the consumer may not notice excessive and unnecessary uses of plastic creeping into the manufacture of consumer items.

We need to discern when plastic is a better material to use than the alternative (plastic chopsticks versus disposable wooden ones), and to distinguish between necessary and superfluous plastic (certain medical uses versus excessive packaging). The best advice I can offer for using plastic is that given by Donella H. Meadows, professor of environmental and policy studies at Dartmouth College: "Recycling is better than disposal, reuse is better than recycling, but reduction is the best of all. It is easier to deal with a flood by turning it off at its source than by inventing better mopping technologies."

RESOURCES

Guide to Action/Organizations

A Citizen's Guide to Plastics in the Ocean: More than a Litter Problem (1988)
Kathryn O'Hara, Suzanne Iudicello, and Rose Bierce
Center for Marine Conservation
1725 DeSales St. NW
Washington, DC 20036
(202) 429-5609
Free

Environmental Defense Fund (EDF)
Wildlife Program
257 Park Avenue South
New York, NY 10010
(212) 505-2100

EDF's wildlife program is working at international and national levels to reduce disposal of plastics at sea and to develop solutions to plastic pollution.

Wrapped in Plastics (1990)
Jeanne Wirka
Environmental Action
1525 New Hampshire Avenue NW
Washington, DC 20036
(202) 745-4870
$10 individuals and nonprofit organizations; $20 government; $30 industry

PART THREE

Drinking Water: Toxins on Tap

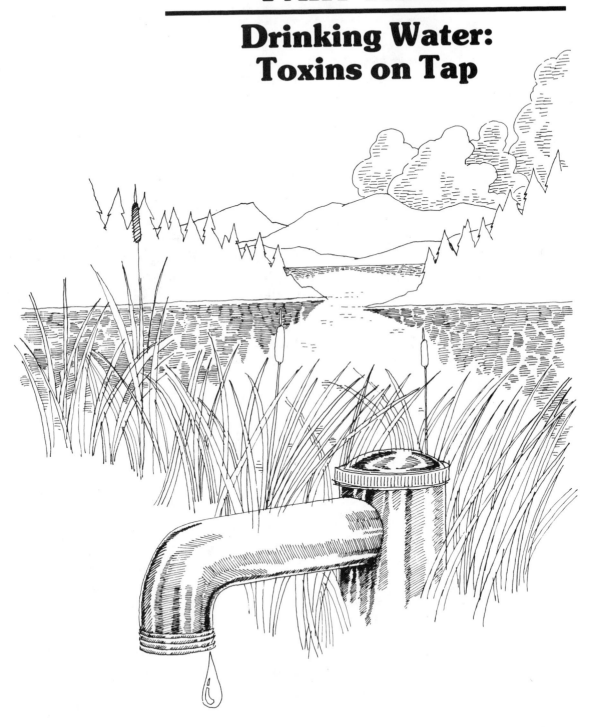

The problem of water pollution . . . can be understood only in context, as part of the whole to which it belongs—the pollution of the entire environment.

Rachel Carson, *Silent Spring* (1962)

*E*arth has been called the water planet. A full three-quarters of the Earth's surface is covered with water—lakes, rivers, bays, wetlands, and mammoth seas. Beneath much of the one-quarter land mass are huge reserves of groundwater, saturating the pore space of soil and flowing through pipelike fractures and channels in rock. We draw our drinking water from surface and underground sources: lakes, rivers, springs, and aquifers composed of water-bearing sand and gravel formations and rock.

More than half of all U.S. citizens drink water drawn from shallow and deep aquifers. Groundwater supplies most rural households, approximately 75 percent of major cities, and most of Florida. The rest of the population drinks water that is diverted from rivers and lakes and stored in reservoirs. Somewhere between its source and our kitchen faucet, drinking water is collected, often filtered and treated to remove contaminants, and then stored for distribution, as Figure A shows. Until recently, we turned on our kitchen tap confident that the water which flowed from it was clean and safe for drinking, cooking, and washing.

- *Clean* because, we imagined, it originates from a pristine source, separate and remote from industrial pollution.
- *Clean* because, we presumed, the municipal water district tests and purifies the water before distributing it to our homes.
- *Cleaner*, because, we knew, our well is private and our land is rural.

But public confidence that water on tap in our homes is, *and will*

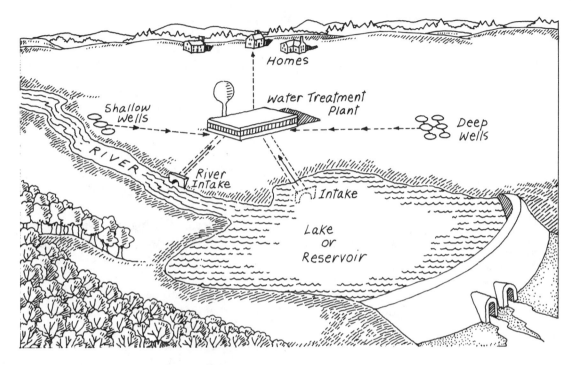

Figure A Public Drinking Water Sources

continue to be, clean and safe is shaken. Nationwide, one in fifteen households now uses bottled water for drinking and cooking; in California, one in three households does. All states are reporting some groundwater contamination from human activities, such as landfills, agriculture and lawn care, septic systems, underground storage tanks, and accidental spills, according to a 1988 report on national groundwater by the U.S. Geological Survey.

Not long ago the largest national conservation organization polled its members to identify the environmental issue most critical to them. The majority replied that drinking water quality concerns them more than any other issue. Responding to that concern, the organization spent eighteen months reviewing the performance of public water systems over the period of one federal fiscal year, October 1986 – September 1987. In its subsequent report, *Danger on*

Tap, the National Wildlife Federation concludes that the government is failing to protect our public drinking water from contamination. They found more than 100,000 violations of federal public health standards and of water testing and reporting standards. These violations affected 40 million individuals drinking community-supplied water as well as water in hotels, factories, and campgrounds. Only two out of every 100 violations were subject to enforcement action and fines. In 94 percent of the cases, people were not notified when their drinking water either was contaminated or had not been adequately tested for contamination.

I was not surprised to find that the majority of the National Wildlife Federation members picked drinking water quality as their highest environmental concern. During the years that I worked in the hazardous waste division of the EPA, the most passionate—and desperate—letters, calls, and protests we received came from people whose water supply was endangered. One morning in 1984, fifty people appeared at my office cubicle with their attorney. The public well that served their five-year-old condominium association had recently become contaminated with chemicals leaching from a nearby commercial landfill. (The landfill would soon be declared a Superfund site.) Unable to sell their units, they could not leave. Relative newcomers in their town, they received no sympathy from the selectmen, who lived elsewhere and felt no urgency to develop a new public water supply. The landfill owners denied any responsibility for the contamination (the studies proving their liability would take years to complete) and would give no financial assistance for alternate water supply. These people had nowhere else to turn except to federal and state agencies, both of which work in time frames of five to ten years for problems of this magnitude. During the next six months I was able to get a temporary water line installed (water was trucked in until the line was in place) and to initiate the five-year process to obtain a permanent water supply. It was the kind of herculean effort, muddled by sleazy local politicians and banal bureaucratic procedures, that burns people out. The condo residents, however, were a key factor in turning around their situation: They were organized, informed, and tenacious, and they never let up.

"What," you may be asking, "can I do to protect my drinking

water against growing contamination of groundwater and slackening government vigilance of public water supplies?" Just as the condo owners had limited options, there are many things you *cannot* do. You cannot, for example, set new and stricter standards for safe concentrations of chemicals in drinking water. You cannot increase the enforcement budget of public drinking water agencies. You cannot undo past spills and disposal of chemicals into the environment.

But you are not powerless to help preserve the quality of your public or private drinking water supply. You can take action in five key ways. All these activities require work, more work than the other issues presented in *EarthRight*. But if preventing pollution begins at home, then drinking water contamination is indeed the place to start.

WHAT YOU CAN DO

1. Understand where your drinking water originates.

2. Identify the potential sources of pollution to your drinking water supply. Minimize your use and disposal of toxic substances.

3. Know whether the water you drink is tested in accordance with the Safe Drinking Water Act, the federal law governing public drinking water, passed in 1974 with subsequent amendments.

4. Investigate alternatives to your current drinking water.

5. Work in your community for by-laws to protect the public water supply from current and future contamination.

Chapter 7

The Origins of Drinking Water

As I write, a mix of wet snow and rain beats rhythmically against my window. This local precipitation is part of a global water cycle that moves water from sea to land and back to sea again. As Figure 7.1 shows, the world's supply of fresh water comes almost entirely from precipitation. Moisture evaporates from the sea, and air masses carry the vapor over the continents. When the vapor cools to its dew point, it condenses to visible water droplets that form clouds or fog. Favorable atmospheric conditions cause some tiny droplets to enlarge and fall to earth as rain, snow, freezing rain, sleet, and hail.

The underground aquifers and the surface rivers and lakes that provide our cities, towns, and private wells with drinking water are constantly fed by the volumes of water lifted from the sea, moved by wind over land, and redeposited on land as rain, snow, or ice. About two-thirds of what reaches land surfaces returns to the atmosphere by evaporation from land surfaces and soil and through transpiration, the giving off of water vapor and photosynthesis byproducts by plants. The remaining water seeps into soil, recharging shallow and deep aquifers, and flows overland into downgradient streams, lakes, and rivers, replenishing reservoirs of surface water. Ultimately, water completes its cycle. Underground water seeps into streams and lakes and returns through these surface channels to the sea.

Walking in the country after a heavy rainstorm offers a lesson in hydrology and, ultimately, drinking water protection. Rain pours off the land and rushes to downhill streams, which feed a common

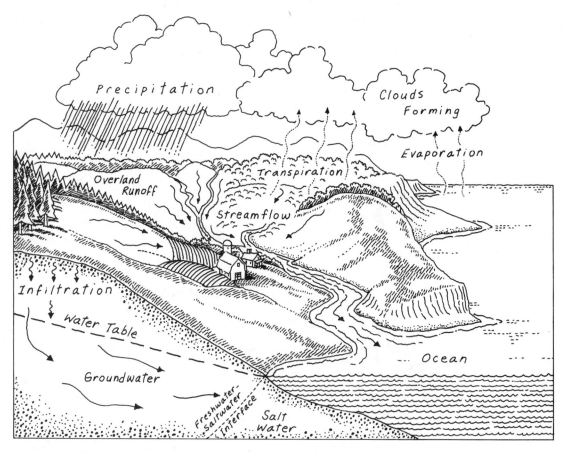

Figure 7.1 The Water Cycle

river. The land from which precipitation drains to a regional river or lake is called a *watershed* or drainage basin (see Figure 7.2).

More and more frequently, signs along highways warn that the adjacent land is a watershed and protected by hazardous materials regulations. These signs tell us two things: (1) Rainfall and other precipitation in the watershed may supply a public drinking water source, and (2) transporters of hazardous materials on local roads and highways are warned to handle their materials carefully to

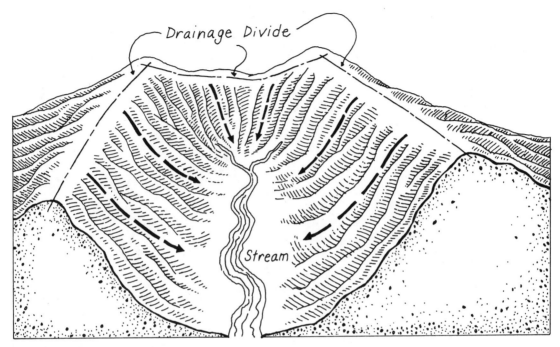

Figure 7.2 Watershed
A watershed, or drainage basin, is a land area that drains surface runoff to
a stream, river, pond, or lake. Coastal watersheds drain to the ocean.

Courtesy of the Massachusetts Audubon Society, Community Groundwater Protection
Project.

avoid spilling or leaking materials that would contaminate the
watershed.

Groundwater flows within a watershed beneath the surface of the
ground, fed by precipitation that falls on the watershed and seeps
into the soil to the water table. Groundwater exists underground almost everywhere—close to the surface of the earth in some places
and thousands of feet deep in others. Like the surface water runoff
after a rainstorm that fills streams that feed rivers, groundwater is
also interconnected to regional surface water. Moving by the force
of gravity away from the *recharge area* (see Figure 7.3), where it is
fed or replenished, groundwater ultimately empties into a stream,
pond, river, or lake.

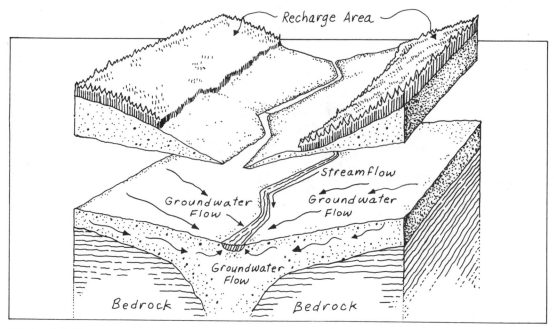

Figure 7.3 Groundwater Recharge Area
Groundwater flows from the recharge areas down to the stream, where it discharges. The stream flows down the valley of the watershed toward the ocean.

Courtesy of the Massachusetts Audubon Society, Community Groundwater Protection Project.

Groundwater is a critical resource both because it provides drinking water and also because it is integrally connected with lakes, rivers, and streams. Groundwater is the source of about 40 percent of the annual average streamflow in the United States. During extended dry periods, groundwater discharges provide nearly all of the base streamflow in drought-affected areas. Invisible and therefore susceptible to unnoticed underground spills, leaks, and disposal of toxic materials, groundwater needs increasing protection.

If your town or city water supply comes from a public well, the pumping well changes the direction of groundwater flow in a portion of the watershed around the well. The groundwater within the

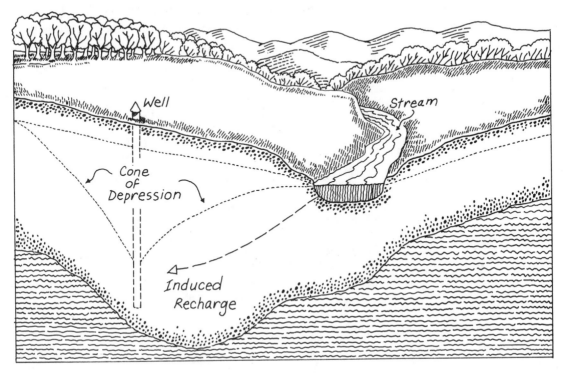

Figure 7.4 Cone of Depression
Pumping a public water supply well may draw recharge from a nearby
stream.

Courtesy of the Massachusetts Audubon Society, Community Groundwater Protection
Project.

influence of the pump flows toward the well and is drawn into the
well. This lowers the groundwater level around the well in the
shape of a cone. The cone-shaped area around the well is called a
cone of depression. A well draws water from only a portion of the
watershed, specifically defined by the cone of depression. As Figure 7.4 shows, a cone of depression may reach as far as a nearby
stream and draw stream water into the well.

The areas critical to drinking water supplies—watershed, recharge area, cone of depression, and surface water—are all susceptible to contamination. They must be identified and then protected

from contamination if we are to keep drinking water clean and safe. Chapter 11 discusses how a community can do this, but let us look first at common human activities that pollute drinking water.

RESOURCES

Reading/Information

Community Groundwater Protection Project
Massachusetts Audubon Society
South Great Rd.
Lincoln, MA 01773
(617) 259-9500

Project publishes a series of information flyers on groundwater protection. Flyer 1 (1984–85) is "An Introduction to Groundwater and Aquifers." $2.25/flyer

Homeowner's Guide to Water Wells (1985)
Kathryn P. Sevebeck
Virginia Water Resources Research Center
Virginia Polytechnic Institute and State University
617 North Main St.
Blacksburg, VA 24060-3397
(703) 231-2600
$6

Story of Drinking Water—Teacher Guides
American Water Works Association
Information Services Department
6666 West Quincy Ave.
Denver, CO 80235
(303) 794-7711
$6.50/guide

These guides (primary, intermediate, and advanced) complement booklets for school-age children that explain the water cycle, drinking water treatment and distribution. Available in Spanish.

Your Water/Your Life (1988)
Public Interest Video Network
1642 R Street NW
Washington, DC 20009
(202) 797-8997

Provides overview of water cycle, aquifers, and sources of contamination of public and private wells. Shows how citizens are responding to contamination of groundwater supplies. Special discount for community organizations. $29.95

Chapter 8

Contamination: How It Happens

S ince 1950, the United States has doubled its industrial production. What does this have to do with your water supply? The model of industrial development is to take air, water, metals, minerals, and fossil fuel resources from nature and to give back "junk." With industrial growth, an increasing amount of toxic industrial chemicals are stored, transported, used, and disposed of, sometimes adjacent to residential neighborhoods, often within a watershed. Groundwater is a subsurface reservoir for rainwater and snow, but increasingly it is also a sink for pollutants carried through the soil with rain and melting snow.

Consider these examples:

- The soil, roadways, and parking lots surrounding a ceramics industry are layered with lead contamination that has settled out from industrial air emissions. Rain washes the lead dust to collection basins and gutters that empty into an unlined industrial settling pond and an adjacent river. The lead dust on soil seeps with rain water deeper into the soil and reaches groundwater.

- A pesticide sprayed on a potato field leaves residue within the recharge area of a farm well. The residue washes through the soil into groundwater and is drawn into the farmer's drinking water well.

- A truck carrying hazardous liquid materials overturns on the highway in a watershed and spills its chemical. Even with immediate cleanup efforts by the truckdriver, fire people, and a local environmental emergency crew, 100 gallons wash into a local river, upstream of the intake for a municipal water supply.

- A small gas station has a twenty-five-year-old underground gasoline storage tank that is steel, unlined, and unprotected from corrosion. A pinhole leak developed three years ago, so minute that the leaking gasoline went undetected until benzene, a component of gasoline, was found in the nearby town well.

Wastes from accidental spills, leaking sewers, salts from urban and highway storm runoff, landfill seepage, air pollution emissions, and wastewater from septic systems, cesspools, and industrial lagoons all migrate into rivers and also into the soil, where they move with groundwater into water supply aquifers. A survey by the Environmental Protection Agency revealed that a third of 26,000 industrial waste ponds regulated by the agency have no liners to prevent chemical liquid wastes from percolating into groundwater. The highest levels of contaminants in soil, groundwater, and surface waters are typically found near landfills, industrial sites, and chemical and fuel storage sites. Since groundwater moves relatively slowly—in some places, a few feet a year; in others, a few feet a day—chemicals spilled or buried at waste sites may not appear in water supply wells located 1 or 2 miles downgradient from a site until decades later.

Tens of thousands of chemicals are used in industry, in laboratories, in agriculture, and in the home. Any of them can spill, settle out from air, or be discharged into the environment, where they may seep into groundwater or wash directly into rivers. The most common contaminants of drinking water are those most frequently used and disposed of within a watershed or recharge area of a drinking water supply. They are chemicals you use regularly.

WATER POLLUTANT 1: ORGANIC SOLVENTS ⸺

Water was the original solvent used to dissolve dirt and grime. But other chemical solvents that dissolve and remove oil, grease, and paint more effectively than water have been employed during this century in enormous quantity to clean clothes, paint equipment, and plastic and metal parts. Some of the most common chemicals found in industrial, domestic, and public water supply wells are synthetic organic solvents with soundalike names, such as tetrachloroethylene, carbon tetrachloride, and trichloroethylene, familiarly called TCE.

How do toxic chemicals get into the water supply? Until recently, used chemical solvents were thrown away rather than being recycled and reused. Valuable when new, they were worthless once spent and dirty. Barrels of waste organic solvent were buried in town landfills and in trenches on industry property. Or waste chemical liquid was poured and piped into pits, ponds, and lagoons to seep out of sight. Barrel- and truck-washing liquids contaminated with solvent residues were routinely discharged at the wash site. Accidental spills were washed into drains that emptied into a nearby stream. Waste oils, sometimes contaminated with PCBs or dioxins, were torched in open pits and sprayed on roadsides for "dust control." These repugnant disposal activities were universal industrial practice for decades until the mid-1970s.

But organic solvents are not limited to the industrial workplace. Many household cleaners contain these same chemicals, including stain and spot removers, degreasers, paint and varnish removers, drain cleaners, and septic system cleaners. How often people thoughtlessly empty a jar of old paint remover down the drain and into the septic system, into a nearby ditch, or in a corner of their yard! Once we understand the general principles of the water cycle and drinking water sources, can we ever use and discard hazardous materials without thinking through the environmental consequences? Knowing the small but sure connections between our use of hazardous chemicals and our drinking water is one key to living more responsibly.

WATER POLLUTANT 2: GASOLINE AND PETROLEUM PRODUCTS

More than 1 million large tanks that store gasoline, petroleum products, and other chemicals lie underground. One expert from the petroleum industry estimates that nearly one-third of the country's 1.2 million gas station tanks—or 400,000 tanks—may be leaking. The largest water production well in Provincetown, Massachusetts had to be shut down in the early 1980s when gasoline from a small service station's underground storage tank was found 600 feet from the well. The town has spent $5 million to partially restore the wellfield.

Many gasoline tanks were installed twenty-five to thirty years ago. Fabricated of steel, unprotected from corrosion, and lacking a secondary container, they corrode and leak through small holes and cracks. Only small amounts of toxic products are needed to contaminate large quantities of potable water. **One gallon of spilled toxic chemical can render 1 million gallons of water unsafe for drinking.** This ratio of minute concentrations of toxic product to enormous quantities of water demonstrates how vigilant we must be to protect our water resources.

WATER POLLUTANT 3: PESTICIDES

Pesticides stand apart from other chemicals. They are designed to kill: Insects, plants, fungi, and rodents are their targets. Many pesticides are so acutely dangerous that they carry detailed precautions for farm workers, gardeners, and any other users about exposure. Since 1962, when Rachel Carson documented the pollution of ecosystems from pesticides and warned about the consequences for drinking water aquifers of pesticide-intensive agriculture and silviculture, pesticide use has increased fivefold in the United States. Forty-five years of substantial pesticide use in the United States has made Carson's prediction of contaminated drinking water supplies come true.

The Environmental Protection Agency recently reports that seventy-four different pesticides have been found in groundwater in thirty-eight states, with agricultural regions the most contaminated. Not only does the routine use of pesticides cause pollution, but so also do accidental spills, throwing away rinsewater from pesticide mixing, and backsiphoning into wells during pesticide mixing and irrigation. Yet even with pesticide pollution prominent in the public news, pesticide sales continue to grow, especially sales of weedkillers. Who are the consumers and users of pesticides?

The agricultural industry accounts for the largest use of pesticides. Utility and railway companies and towns routinely spray herbicides on rights-of-way. Pesticides are also used for mosquito and gypsy moth control by towns and cities. But homeowners account for a large percentage of pesticide use. One environmental group estimates that 40 percent of the pesticide products on the market are intended for home use. The National Academy of Sciences finds that homeowners use approximately 85 million pounds of pesticides per year. This amounts to 5 to 10 pounds per acre, a rate of use on suburban lawns and gardens which exceeds that applied to most other land areas in the country!

Nor can we take comfort in the fact that these chemicals are registered by the government. Many "registered" chemicals have not been fully tested for toxicity. Of the 35,000 pesticides registered for use, public drinking water standards have been set for only six. Public drinking water supplies are not routinely tested for even these six pesticides. And private well owners are under no obligation to test for these chemicals. As mentioned earlier, **using toxic chemicals for a "pristine" lawn is a recent suburban practice that is profoundly unecological.** For how can pesticides be sprayed and dusted in yard and garden without ultimately becoming part of the water cycle that is intimately connected with soil?

WATER POLLUTANT 4: ROAD SALT

Every winter in snowbelt states, road salt mixed with sand is spread on public roads to melt snow and ice. Most of the salt used is sodium chloride. The water-soluble sodium chloride either runs off roadways dissolved in melted ice and snow to nearby lakes and streams or it percolates into groundwater. Recharge areas for public water supply and private wells are likely to be contaminated from high sodium levels if they are crisscrossed by highways on which road salt is heavily used.

Excessive salt can contribute to hypertension, and high sodium levels pose a threat to those with heart, liver, or kidney ailments. At a time when so many people are cutting intake of salt in their diet, this problem increasingly plagues many water supplies. **Although water naturally contains some sodium, road salt contamination of groundwater has significantly increased in the last thirty years.** Federal and state limits for sodium in drinking water are 20 parts per million (ppm). In the state of Massachusetts, the salt in almost one-third of public water supplies has exceeded that limit. Perhaps more serious than the annual salting of highways is the stockpiling of salt-sand mixtures. To a lesser extent, the same is true of snowdumping from snowplowing of city streets. If stockpiles of salt and salt-laden snow are located over recharge areas and near wells, the potential for drinking water contamination is especially high.

WATER POLLUTANT 5: COMMERCIAL FERTILIZERS ———

The nitrogen cycle—in which nitrogen is taken in by plants that are eaten by animals that return nitrogen to soil, all assisted by bacteria—is essential. Like pesticides, commercial fertilizers have been used increasingly on crops, lawns and golf courses in the past forty years. Nitrogen in fertilizer is oxidized to nitrates that dissolve in water and move through soil into groundwater. High nitrate levels in groundwater come from many sources of nitrogen in addition to commercial fertilizers: animal feedlot waste, septic systems, leaking sewer lines, and landfill seepage. If any of these sources is located in the recharge area and seeps into a water supply or washes into a surface water body, it can increase the level of nitrates in drinking water above the federal standard (10 ppm). Nitrate levels greater than 50 ppm are a health threat especially to infants, having been known to cause methemoglobinemia, or "blue baby" syndrome, which can be fatal. They can also contribute to the formation of cancer-causing compounds, nitrosamines.

WATER POLLUTANT 6: SEPTIC SYSTEMS

Septic systems are small wastewater treatment plants where bacteria break down human waste into simpler components and destroy many harmful bacteria and viruses. Large wastewater treatment plants usually discharge the treated wastewater into a nearby river, whereas septic systems recharge local groundwater. Even well-designed septic systems release some bacteria and nitrates into the ground, with the septic liquid piped to the leachfield. Effluent from septic systems can also contain the toxic chemicals of whatever has been poured down the drain: metals from photoprocessing, organic chemicals from paint remover and furniture stripping, and waste oil and gasoline, for example. Even chemical septic system cleaners, containing hazardous chemicals that cannot be destroyed in the septic system, have contaminated nearby wells.

The most important factors in keeping septic systems efficient in cleaning wastewater and keeping wastewater from contaminating the water supply are a mix of human practices: no disposal of toxic wastes in the system, along with proper design and location of the septic system and well. Where many septic systems are located within the cone of depression of a public water supply, there is an increased chance for contamination.

WATER POLLUTANT 7: DUMPS AND LANDFILLS

On a map of your town or city, mark the currently used landfill and all former landfills and dumps. These points locate some of the most critical sources of pollution to local groundwater and to public water supplies, if they lie within the recharge area. Until recently, landfills were large holes in the ground where any kind of waste could be dumped and covered. Often towns used an abandoned sand and gravel pit as a landfill; landfill liquid, wastewater, waste oil, and septic wastes would leach quickly through the permeable sandy soil. It was not uncommon for tank trucks to pump their liquid wastes into these porous pits.

All landfills and dumps generate a liquid called *leachate*. Leachate is a brew of those soluble chemicals present in the house garbage, office waste, demolition waste, and often industrial waste mixed together with biological waste in the landfill. Rain filters into the landfill and dissolves soluble material that mixes with liquid waste. Landfill leachate trickles through the layers of waste and out the unlined bottom and sides. Often decades pass, during which time a landfill is filled, sealed, and closed, before the leachate is discovered seeping from the base or mixing with water that recharges a water supply.

WATER POLLUTANT 8: LEAD

Lead is a toxic metal that was used in many consumer products including house paint, gasoline, water pipes, and solder for copper pipes. Young children, infants, and fetuses are especially vulnerable to lead poisoning, which can irreversibly affect both their mental and physical development. Unlike the other sources of contamination, lead in drinking water most often comes from within the water system. Typically, lead gets into water after the water leaves the municipal water plant or well. The source of lead is most likely lead pipe or lead solder in the plumbing of your home that corrodes and dissolves into water. Some conditions increase the amount of lead that concentrates in your water from lead pipes or lead solder—for instance, water standing in the pipes for many hours, hot tap water, and "soft" water.

Lead-contaminated drinking water is most often a problem in very old and very new houses. Plumbing installed before 1930, including interior plumbing and service connections that join house pipes to public water supplies, most likely contains lead. Copper pipes have replaced lead pipes in most residential plumbing. Until June 1988, however, lead solder was used with copper pipes. The Environmental Protection Agency estimates that lead solder in new pipes dissolves into water for a period of about five years.

The mechanisms by which drinking water becomes contaminated with toxic chemicals are often simple; understanding and undoing the harm are complex and costly. Figure 8.1 conveys the multiple potential sources of contamination of a public water supply. Within the cone of depression and recharge area of a municipal well are located unlined waste dumps, industrial ponds, manure

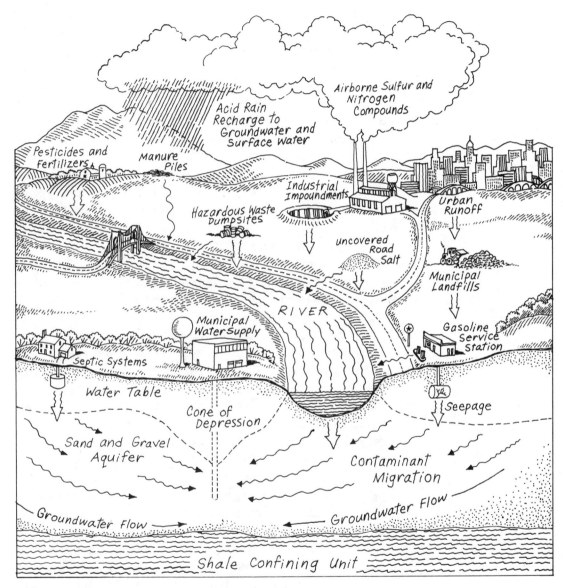

Figure 8.1 Sources of Groundwater Contamination

and salt piles, and leaking underground septic and gasoline tanks. Airborne industrial and agricultural chemicals settle out and mix with rain, then wash into soil overlying the aquifer. In time, pollutants and leachate seep through the soil, enter the groundwater, and move with it toward the pumping well. Surface water runoff carries dissolved salt, nitrates, pesticides, and leaking waste from corroding drums into the nearby river upstream of the municipal well. The pumping well draws some river water into the water supply.

The complexities of contamination enter with the following factors: the kinds of chemicals in the landfill; the amount and type of soil under the landfill; the chemical strength of the leachate; the dilution by groundwater and river water; the rate of flow of groundwater; and the relationship of the chemicals to water. A gasoline leak from an underground storage tank will float on top of the water, being lighter than water and insoluble with it, with some of its constituents dissolving slightly in groundwater and river water. A heavy, dense fuel, on the other hand, will sink through groundwater and move along the bottom of the aquifer. Some metals, pesticides, and other organic chemicals will attach to soil particles for chemical or physical reasons, and will not initially migrate into groundwater until the holding capacity of the soil is saturated. In some cases plants will take up contaminants bound to soil in their root zone. Soil bacteria can break down certain organic compounds, either to harmless chemicals or to other toxic, sometimes more harmful chemicals. Some chemicals, such as chlorides and metals, resist any degradation.

Water-soluble pollutants that are discharged or washed into a lake or river usually disperse throughout the water body, mix with the water, and become dilute. Groundwater, in contrast to surface water, moves slowly and has little mixing. Pollutants in groundwater usually form a slug of concentrated contamination and move as a plume with groundwater. This fact—that contaminants are concentrated and not fully dispersed and mixed in groundwater—does allow for tracking the plume and treating groundwater where contamination is most concentrated. **But it is difficult, very expensive, and sometimes impossible to correct groundwater pol-**

lution. **Preventing contamination is a much sounder environmental and economic policy.**

RESOURCES

Reading/Information

Community Groundwater Protection Project
Groundwater Information Flyer 2, "Groundwater
Contamination: From the Watershed into the Well" (1984–85)
Massachusetts Audubon Society
South Great Rd.
Lincoln, MA 01773
(617) 259-9500
$2.25

Groundwater Protection: Saving the Unseen Resource
Guide to Problems, Causes and Government Responses (1987)
Conservation Foundation
1250 24th Street NW
Washington, DC 20037
(202) 293-4800
$15

Groundwater and the Rural Homeowner (1988)
U.S. Geological Survey
Federal Center, Box 25425
Denver, CO 80225
No charge

Homeowner's Guide to Septic Systems (1985)
Torsten D. Sponenberg; Jacob H. Kahn; K.P. Sevebeck
Publication Services
Virginia Water Resources Research Center
Virginia Polytechnic Institute and State University
617 North Main St.
Blacksburg, VA 24060-3397
(703) 231-3600
$6

Lead and Your Drinking Water (1987)
EPA Public Information Center
401 M Street SW
Washington, DC 20460
(202) 475-7751
No charge

Organic Chemicals and Drinking Water (1980)
Nancy Kim and Daniel Stone
New York State Department of Health
Bureau of Public Water Supply
Empire State Plaza
Tower Building Room 482
Albany, NY 12237
(518) 474-2121
Price not given

Pesticides and Groundwater: Pesticides as Potential Pollutants (1988)
Thomas J. Bicid
University of Illinois, Urbana-Champaign
College of Agriculture
Cooperative Extension Service
Urbana, IL 61801
(217) 333-4666
Price not given

Chapter 9

Testing Your Drinking Water

Almost 4,000 years ago, a Sanskrit document instructed its readers that storing water in copper vessels, exposing it to sunlight, and filtering it through charcoal improves water quality. Yet only since the late nineteenth century, when the Lawrence Experiment Station of the Massachusetts Board of Health demonstrated that slow sand filtration of water reduced the death rate from typhoid by 79 percent, has public drinking water been tested and treated in the United States. Throughout the twentieth century, people have trusted that, even if water pumped from groundwater or from a lake or river to holding tanks were initially contaminated, public drinking water arrives in our homes filtered, disinfected, and safe to use. Here is a typical series of treatment steps that water may undergo before it is distributed to your home.

- Water is drawn from surface and groundwater sources to storage areas. Copper sulfate is added to control algal growth.
- Water is filtered to remove debris.
- A chemical such as alum is added to coagulate unfiltered particles.
- Water moves slowly through sedimentation basins while solid coagulated particles sink to the bottom.
- Water flows through sand and gravel beds for final filtering.
- Chlorine is added as a disinfectant to kill bacteria.

- Water is treated to make it less corrosive to lead pipes and solder.

After treatment, the water is tested for biological and chemical contaminants, as required by the Environmental Protection Agency and state drinking water regulations. The treated water is stored in holding tanks or reservoirs for distribution.

The federal Safe Water Drinking Act and similar state statutes oblige the EPA and the state drinking water agencies to identify the chemical and bacteriological pollutants that can contaminate water and threaten public health. The agencies establish a maximum level for specific contaminants, MCL for short, meaning the highest level of a specific contaminant that is permissible in drinking water. Each public water authority must test for these contaminants on a scheduled basis, treat the water if any contaminants are found above the MCL, and notify the public when it receives water from a system in violation of the law. In other words, people must be notified by their water supplier in either of these situations:

- If their water has not been tested for all required contaminants,

- If their water has levels of contaminants above an MCL.

This is the theoretical public system of providing safe drinking water. What is the reality?

Reality is this: **The EPA identified over a thousand likely sources of contamination in drinking water**, according to the Center for Science in the Public Interest. Mainly chemicals, these contaminants find their way into drinking water supplies through the multiple pathways we have considered: leaking underground storage tanks, fertilizer and pesticide use, lead pipes, salt use and storage, industrial discharge into a river, air pollution, and landfill and septic system leachate. Of these 1,000 possible pollutants, the EPA requires, through state authority in most cases, public water utilities to test for up to thirty on a scheduled basis and to monitor up to thirty-six others. Table 9.1 shows the thirty chemicals for which drinking water standards have been set, the probable sources of the contaminants, and their possible health effects. The 1986 amendments to the Safe Drinking Water Act require the EPA to establish maximum contaminant levels for another eighty-three chemicals. In addition, your state agency may require testing for other chemicals—for example, for a specific pesticide that has been found in local drinking water systems.

Table 9.1 Primary Drinking Water Standards

Contaminants	Health Effects	MCL	Sources
Microbiological			
Total coliforms (coliform bacteria fecal coliform, steptococcal and other bacteria)	Not necessarily disease-producing themselves, but coliforms can be indicators of organisms that cause assorted gastroenteric infections; giardiasis, shigellosis, camplyobacterosis, hepatitis A, salmonellosis, and general gastroenteritis	1 per 100 milliliters	Human and animal fecal matter.
Turbidity	Interferes with disinfection	1-5tu	Erosion, runoff, and sediment discharges.
Inorganic chemicals		*mg/l*	
Arsenic	Dermal and nervous system toxicity effects, possible cancer risk	.05	Pesticide residues, industrial waste and smelter operations. Geological.
Barium	A variety of cardiac, gastrointestinal and neuromuscular effects	1	Coal-fired power plants, filler for automotive paints, and specialty compounds used in bricks, tiles and jet fuels. Geological.
Cadmium	Kidney effects producing renal dysfunction, hypertension, anemia and altered liver microsomal activity	.01	Mining, smelting, fossil fuel use, fertilizer application, and sewage sludge. Geological.
Chromium	Liver/kidney effects	.05	Abandoned mining operations and electroplating operations. Geological.
Lead	Central and peripheral nervous system damage. Kidney effects. Highly toxic to infants and pregnant women. Impaired mental performance in children	.02	Leaches from lead pipe and lead based solder pipe joints. Airborne lead from gasoline combustion.
Mercury	Central nervous system disorders; kidney effects	.002	Used in manufacture of paint, paper, vinyl chloride. Used in fungicides. Geological.
Nitrate	Methemoglobinemia ("blue baby syndrome") which results in asphyxia, cancer risk	10	Fertilizer, sewage, feedlots, geological.
Selinium	Gastrointestinal effects	.01	Coal burning, mining, smelting, selenium refining, glass manufacture, and fuel oil combustion. Geological.

(continued)

Table 9.1 Primary Drinking Water Standards (continued)

Contaminants	Health Effects	MCL	Sources
Silver	Skin discoloration (argyria)	.05	Mining and processing. Geological.
Fluoride	Skeletal damage	4	Additive to drinking water, toothpaste, foods processed with fluoridated water. Geological.
Organic chemicals			
Endrin	Nervous system/kidney effects	.0002	Insecticide used on cotton, small grains and orchards (canceled).
Lindane	Nervous system, kidney and liver effects; possible cancer risk	.004	Insecticide used on seed and soil treatments, foilage applications, wood protection.
Methoxychlor	Nervous system/kidney effects	.1	Insecticide used on fruit trees, vegetables.
2, 4-D	Liver/kidney effects	.1	Herbicide used to control broadleaf weeds in agriculture, used on forests, range, pastures, and aquatic environments.
2,4,5-TP Silvex	Liver/kidney effects	.01	Herbicide, canceled in 1984.
Toxaphene	Cancer risk	.005	Insecticide used on cotton, corn, grain.
*Benzene	Cancer causing	.005	Fuel (leaking tanks), solvents commonly used in manufacture of industrial chemicals, pharmaceuticals, pesticides, paints, and plastics.
*Carbon tetrachloride	Possible cancer risk	.005	Common in cleaning agents and industrial wastes from manufacture of coolants.
*p-Dichloro-benzene	Possible cancer risk	.075	Used in insecticides, moth balls, and air deodorizers.
*1,2-Dichloro-ethane	Possible cancer risk	.005	Used in manufacture of insecticides.
*1,1-Dichloro-ethylene	Liver/kidney effects	.007	Used in manufacture of plastics, dyes, perfumes, paints, and SOCs.
*1,1,1-Trichloro-ethane	Nervous system effects	.2	Used in manufacture of food wrappings, synthetic fibers.
*Trichloroethane	Possible cancer risk	.005	Waste from disposal of dry cleaning materials. From manufacture of pesticides, paints, waxes and varnishes, paint stripper, and metal degreaser.

(continued)

Table 9.1   Primary Drinking Water Standards (continued)

Contaminants	Health Effects	MCL	Sources
*Vinyl Chloride	Cancer risk	.002	Polyvinylchloride pipes (PVC) and solvents used to join them. Industrial waste from manufacture of plastics and synthetic rubber.
Total trihalomethanes			
(TTHM) (chloroform, bromoform, bromodichloromethane, dibromochloromethane)	Cancer risk	.1	Primarily formed when surface water containing organic matter is treated with chlorine.
Radionuclides			
Gross alpha particle activity	Cancer causing	15 pCi/l	Radioactive waste, uranium deposits.
Gross beta particle activity	Cancer causing	4 mrem/yr	Radioactive waste, uranium deposits.
Radium 226 & 228 (total)	Cancer causing	5 pCi/l	Radioactive waste, geological.

*Effective January 9, 1989.

tu	=	turbidity unit.
mg/l	=	1 milligram per liter or 1 unit of weight or volume of a material in 1 million units of water.
pC/l	=	1 picoCurie of radiation in 1 liter of water.
mrem/yr	=	1 millirem of radiation in one year.

SOURCE: "You and Your Drinking Water," *EPA Journal* vol. 12, no. 7 (September 1986).

Altogether, then, public drinking water is required by federal law to be tested routinely for less than 10 percent of possible contaminants. At the same time, the U.S. Geological Survey reports that toxic constituents and synthetic organic chemicals have contaminated shallow aquifers in many parts of the country. The USGS warns that reports of contamination will increase as the search intensifies and more sophisticated techniques of detection are used. That is one element of reality.

Another is the record of enforcement by public drinking water agencies. In their report *Danger on Tap*, the National Wildlife Federation found that nearly half of the 201,000 public water systems in the United States violated the Safe Drinking Water Act during fiscal year 1987 in one of three ways:

1. Exceeding public health standards (the MCLs) for a contaminant(s).
2. Failing to test for all required contaminants and report the results.
3. Failing to notify customers when the system was in violation of the law.

These violations affected the drinking water of about one in six people who, with few exceptions, were not informed of the violations.

The National Wildlife Federation strongly recommends that the EPA and the states hold *all* public water systems and corporate officials accountable for *all* violations of safe drinking water regulations, and not just prosecute a few to warn the rest. The federal and state budgets for drinking water enforcement activities, however, are relatively small and marginal compared to other programs. They reflect neither the serious hazard to health in unsafe drinking water nor the priority of the issue for all citizens. In the absence of sufficient public resources and political will to protect drinking water, it is all the more critical that we be informed and take action where we can.

WHAT YOU CAN DO

1. Obtain Test Results.

If your drinking water is provided by a public system, you can obtain the results of obligatory water testing from your community water company or water authority. All public water systems are required to test on a scheduled basis for specific contaminants for which the EPA has established standards. Records must be kept of these tests, and test results must be reported to the government regulatory agency. By law, your water provider must give you the

---

KNOW YOUR DRINKING WATER

1. Write your water supplier.

2. Request the list and schedule of water quality tests required by EPA and the state.

3. Request water quality results for previous 12 months.

4. Compare results with Table 9.1.

5. Consult state water supply office if water is contaminated.

---

results of its testing, if you request them. Keep in mind that although the federal Safe Drinking Water Act requires *all* public water systems to test for *all* contaminants in Table 9.1 on a scheduled basis, the EPA does not. Most public water systems are required by the EPA and the state drinking water agency to test for a limited number of the contaminants in Table 9.1 on a regular basis. In the written request to your water supplier for test results, also ask for the list and schedule of water quality tests required by the EPA and the state agency.

You can obtain a list of standards for new contaminants and their MCLs added to the original list of thirty MCLs, and also any "health advisories" or guidelines for contaminants that as yet have no standards, from the EPA Safe Drinking Water Hotline at (800) 426-4791. Your state drinking water agency can provide you with standards for any contaminants they regulate in addition to those required by the EPA. Once you have received a copy of your local drinking water test results, compare them with the EPA standards in Table 9.1 and any new standards subsequently set by the EPA and your state. This is a first step toward knowing the quality of your drinking water.

2. Know When to Test Your Water.

There are a number of contexts in which you should consider having your drinking water tested.

- **Your drinking water is from a private well or an unregu-lated water system and you have a septic system.** No authority requires regular testing of water systems that have fewer than fifteen service connections and serve fewer than twenty-five people. If there are no sources of chemical pollution, such as local pesticide use, nearby industry, or road salt, then the major potential source of contamination is the septic system. A test for coliform bacteria and ni-trates will indicate whether septic waste has infected your water supply.

- **You suspect the presence of lead** from either lead pipes, lead service connections, or lead solder on copper pipes. The laboratory must be able to detect lead in water to 20 parts per billion, the new federal standard.

- **There is a change in the color, taste or odor of your water.**

- **Your water company has fewer than 3,300 customers.** Small public utilities have a less rigorous schedule of moni-toring requirements than large ones.

- **Your well is located near a landfill or waste dump, a farm that uses pesticides, an industrial park, a military base, a chemical manufacturing plant, or an underground tank storing hazardous materials.**

There are thousands of possible sources of pollution. How, then, do you know what to test for? It is important to single out the pol-lutants, in addition to those from septic waste, that might migrate to your water supply before you choose the chemicals for testing. Develop a map of the land uses within a 500-foot radius of your well, with special attention to those that are located upgradient, that is, uphill from your well. Although groundwater does not al-ways flow along the same gradient as surface water runoff, it fre-quently does. Under the Emergency Planning and Right-to-Know Law, you can obtain information on hazardous chemicals used by industries and businesses within the radius of concern from the EPA Emergency Planning and Community Right-to-Know Hotline

---

KNOW YOUR DRINKING WATER

1. List problems with water quality and/or chemicals in use nearby.

2. Select EPA-certified laboratory. Discuss tests with laboratory chemist.

3. Compare test results with Table 9.1

4. Consult local board of health if water is contaminated.

---

at (800) 535-0202. Closer to home, your local board of health, planning board, and fire chief may have the same information. For information on pesticide use by farmers and on rights-of-way, call your county agricultural extension service or state pesticide bureau. If you suspect former landfill or buried wastes, the U.S. Geological Survey has overflight maps from as far back as 1930. Your community library also may have archival records with photographs.

Water quality tests are numerous and expensive, so it is necessary to identify the most likely contaminants of concern. Once you have developed a map of the land use around your well and have established the probable direction of recharge for your well water (although this will be less certain than land use), discuss with the laboratory chemist the critical chemicals and biological parameters for which to test. If any contamination is found, the levels should be compared with standards set by the EPA and the state for drinking water contaminants. If levels of contaminants exceed any federal or state standards of health advisories, the water should either not be used or treated to remove contaminants before use, in consultation with the local board of health.

If you decide to use a private testing service, avoid ones that sell purification systems so as to minimize any conflict of interest. Make certain that the laboratory is certified by the EPA for drinking water quality analysis through a program of laboratory certification carried out by your state. Your state drinking water certification officer has a list of approved laboratories in your city or county. The name of the state drinking water certification officer can be gotten by calling the EPA Safe Drinking Water Hotline or your state drinking water agency.

RESOURCES

Guides to Action/Organizations

EPA Emergency Planning and Community Right-to-Know Hotline
(800) 535-0202

Will provide information on hazardous chemicals used by local businesses.

EPA Safe Drinking Water Hotline
(800) 426-4791

Will provide lists of final and proposed federal standards for regulated contaminants and "health advisories" or guidelines for contaminants that have no standards. State water protection agency will give the same information for additional contaminants regulated by the state.

Reading/Information

Danger on Tap: the Government's Failure to Enforce the Federal Safe Drinking Water Act (1988)
National Wildlife Federation
1400 16th Street NW
Washington, DC 20036
(202) 797-6800
Free

Interpreting Drinking Water Quality Analysis: What Do the Numbers Mean (1980)
Theodore B. Shelton, PhD
Cooperative Extension Service
Cook College
Rutgers, the State University of New Jersey
New Brunswick, NJ 08903
(201) 932-9762
$2

"National Water Summary 1986—Hydrologic Events and Groundwater Quality," USGS Water-Supply Paper 2325 (1988)
U.S. Geological Survey
Books and Open-File Reports Section
Federal Center, Box 25425
Denver, Colorado 80225
$36

Chapter 10

The Alternatives: Bottled Water and Home Treatment

BOTTLED WATER: IS IT BETTER?

Increasingly, people are turning away from the kitchen tap to bottled water for drinking and cooking water. Between 1977 and 1987, U.S. sales of bottled water increased by almost 500 percent to catapult bottled water into a $1.9 billion-a-year industry. At an average price of $0.89 per gallon, bottled water costs nearly 700 times the average cost of tap water. Imported water costs three times the cost of oil!

Some people have no choice but to use bottled water. They are forced to rely on it when their private wells or public water supplies become contaminated at levels that the state or federal government declares unsafe for use. The government routinely turns to bottled water as a "short-term" alternative to contamination of groundwater and surface water drinking supply.

The bottled water industry presents its product as substantially cleaner, fresher, and safer than domestic water supply. Bottled water is packaged to appear as a pure and contaminant-free alternative to tap water. At 700 times the cost of tap water, is bottled water always better than tap water—and worth the markup?

In January 1989, the Environmental Policy Institute answered that question in *Bottled Water: Sparkling Hype at a Premium Price*. After reviewing independent and government studies of bottled water as well as the related state and federal regulations, they concluded that bottled water is not necessarily any safer nor any more healthful than the water that comes out of most faucets. In fact, **one-third of all bottled water in the United States comes from public water utilities—the same ones serving households!** The remaining bottled water comes from the same kinds of sources as public water supplies: groundwater, springs, and surface water.

What of the regulations governing their purity? Bottled water has to meet fewer contaminant standards than does tap water. The results of testing do not have to be reported by the bottled water companies to any federal agency. In other words, the bottling companies are self-policing. The Food and Drug Administration, the federal agency responsible for regulating bottled water, has no monitoring program and admits that bottled water quality is a low priority. Bottled water regulations specifically exempt *mineral waters* from the few water-quality testing standards that do exist. The regulations do not protect against potential contamination from packaging and storage.

Even the bottled water industry trade association, the International Bottled Water Association, has petitioned the FDA to upgrade existing federal regulations. In the absence of such federal guidelines, the trade association has set its own test standards for members and supports stricter regulation at the state level. A small number of states—notably, California, Connecticut, Florida, Massachusetts, New Jersey, and Wisconsin—have adopted regulations more rigorous than those of the FDA that address the problems associated with bottled water quality. These include issues of more and stricter quality tests and standards; mandatory reporting of test results; no exemptions for mineral waters; labeling of source and type of water; and testing before and after water is treated and bottled.

In reviewing studies of bottled water, the Environmental Policy Institute found that bottled water frequently contains low levels of contaminants such as heavy metals and solvents, some of which may come from the processing and storage of the water.

- Thirteen of fourteen out-of-state brands of mineral water sold in Massachusetts exceeded state guidelines for sodium in a 1987 Massachusetts State Department of Health survey. The survey of domestic and foreign bottled water products sold in Massachusetts found that lead, fluoride, trihalomethanes, and radionuclides were present in several products, in some cases in excess of federal and state standards.

● Traces of volatile organic chemicals, although not in excess of federal and state standards, were found in forty-eight of ninety-three bottled waters sampled in a 1987 New York Department of Health survey. Toluene was present in low levels in twenty-eight percent of products tested, although the authors suspect that the toluene came from the bottling process, caps/containers, or labeling operations.

● A survey conducted by the New York Department of Public Water Supply Protection in 1982 examined twenty-two bottled water products for thirty-nine organic chemicals. The study found that 68 percent of the products contained detectable levels of some of the organic chemicals. Some of the bottled water came from a municipal water supply.

● A 1985 study by the California State Assembly's Office of Research reported problems of bottled water "doctored" with chlorine, unsanitary bottling conditions, and bottled water sources located near toxic materials. The report resulted in the most stringent bottled water regulations in the country.

● A 1986 study by the California Department of Health Services concluded that the longer water is stored in plastic bottles made with polycarbonate resins, the higher the concentration of methylene chloride in the water. Storage beyond fourteen days resulted in levels of methylene chloride above the state standard.

The EPI points out that in the majority of studies they reviewed, bottled water is usually in compliance with current federal regulations. As we have seen in some of the previously cited studies, however, this does not mean that bottled water is free of contaminants or superior to your own drinking water. Bottled water may be tap water if the label reads "purified," "distilled," "soda," "club," and, in some cases, "mineral" water. "Spring water" is the excep-

---

KNOW YOUR BOTTLED WATER

1. Write bottled water company. Ask if bottler is member of IBWA.

2. Ask where the water is obtained and how the source is protected against contamination.

3. Ask how water is treated prior to bottling.

4. Request list and schedule of water quality tests and whether water is tested before and after bottling.

5. Request water quality results for previous 12 months.

6. Compare results with Table 9.1.

---

tion; its source is likely to be a spring. Water "purification" may remove some contaminants, not necessarily all. Bottled water is subject to many of the same contamination problems that threaten groundwater and surface water supplies, since it comes from the same types of sources that serve municipal water supplies.

There may be compelling reasons to use bottled water in place of your domestic supply: lead pipes or solder, reports of drinking water contamination in your community, too high sodium in the public supply, contaminated private well, and so on. As with your public water supplier, you can write the bottler—Poland Spring, Evian, Perrier, and others—and request information on their water quality. Three primary issues to ascertain are the water source, water treatment, and water quality tests and test results. Where does the bottler obtain the water? What actions does the bottler take to prevent contamination of the source? What treatment, if any, does the bottler use, and why? For what contaminants is the water tested, and how frequently? Is the water tested after bottling? Does the bottler belong to the International Bottled Water Association (IBWA) and adhere to its requirements for testing? Ask for a copy of the past year's results.

The bottler's address can be found on the product label or obtained from the IBWA. Although it is not obligated to reply to your request for test results, a commercial water company will probably do so. Compare what they test for and their test results to the list of federal standards for drinking water contaminants in Table 9.1 and any new additional standards and advisories, obtained from the EPA hotline and the state.

HOME TREATMENT

Filters and treatment units on home water supplies can be effective in removing organic chemicals and metals as well as filtering out hazardous microbes from drinking water. But they must be selected to solve the specific problem and then maintained; otherwise they can exacerbate the problem. In other words, don't buy a water purifying unit until you know what problem you are trying to solve. Water testing helps define the problem; the results of testing are used in selecting treatment systems.

Table 10.1 provides a general overview of water treatment units, their uses and limitations. You will need to do more in-depth research and consult with specialists who market the units in order to match your specific water quality problems with an effective treatment unit(s). Your local board of health may also be knowledgeable and helpful in choosing appropriate water treatment units. Because of the extensive number of filtration and purification systems available, I have included a list of sources on home treatment systems in the Resources section of this chapter.

ELIMINATING LEAD

There are many practices to reduce or remove lead, ranging from the no-cost practical actions to more expensive technical ones. If your drinking water is contaminated with lead or if you suspect that it is, don't use water that has sat in pipes for 6 hours or more for cooking or drinking. Allow the cold water in each drinking water faucet to run until it has become as cold as it can get. Letting the water run an extra 15 seconds after it cools should also flush the service connector. Once you have flushed a tap, you might fill bot-

Table 10.1   Overview of Home Treatment Devices

Device	Primary Use	Limitations
Carbon filter	Removes chlorine, general taste and odor problems, specific organic chemicals, including some pesticide residues.	Does not remove nitrates, bacteria, or metals. Maintenance necessary.
Reverse osmosis	Removes some organic chemicals, including most pesticides, and heavy metals, including lead.	Does not remove 100% of most chemicals. Uses large amounts of water.
Distillation	Removes minerals such as nitrate and sodium, heavy metals including lead, as well as many organic chemicals. Kills bacteria.	Bland-tasting water. Cleaning necessary.
Chlorination	Kills or reduces bacteria and viruses to safe levels.	Does not remove nitrates or other chemicals. May result in excess chlorine or chlorinated compounds.
Water softener	Replaces water hardness minerals (calcium, magnesium) with sodium. Improves cleaning action of soaps. Prevents scales in water pipes and equipment.	Sodium content in water increased. Softened water can be more corrosive and dissolve lead in pipe or solder. Maintenance necessary.
Neutralizer	Treats acidic water.	May increase sodium content in water.

SOURCE: Adapted from Annette Bach and Darnell Lundstrom, "Quick Reference to Water Treatment Devices," *Household Water Treatment*, North Dakota State University Extension Service, June 1988.

tles with water for cooking and drinking throughout the day. Never cook or consume water from the hot water tap since hot water dissolves lead more quickly than cold water.

If you are served by a public water system, contact the water supplier or district and ask whether the system contains lead piping or if the water is corrosive. If either answer is yes, ask what the supplier is doing about the problem of lead contamination. In some cases, the water is treated to make it less corrosive. In others, water mains containing lead pipes and portions of lead service connections are replaced.

There are a number of commercial systems for the home to make water less corrosive or to remove lead (see Table 10.1 and the Resources section). In homes where lead is a problem, water softeners should not be connected to pipes leading to drinking water taps, since water softeners can contribute to the corrosiveness of water and cause lead to dissolve more rapidly. If you move into a newly built home, remove all strainers from the faucets and flush the water for at least 15 minutes to remove any loose lead solder from the plumbing. Check the strainers occasionally for any accumulation of loose lead. Instruct, in writing, any plumber you hire to use only lead-free materials for repairs and in newly installed plumbing.

RESOURCES

Guides to Action/Organization

"Lead and Your Drinking Water" (April 1987)
EPA Publication EPA-87-006
U.S. Government Printing Office
Washington, DC 20402
Free

Questions to Ask When Purchasing Water Treatment Equipment (1988)
Linda Wagenet and Ann Lemley
Cooperative Extension Service
Cornell University
Ithaca, NY 14853
(607) 255-2116
$0.35

Water Treatment Handbook (1985)
c/o Roger Moyer
513 Fairview St.
Coopersburg, PA 18036
(215) 282-3561
Price unknown

Reading/Information

Bottled Water: Sparkling Hype at a Premium Price (1989)
Sandra Marquardt et al.
The Environmental Policy Institute
218 D St. SE
Washington, DC 20003
(202) 544-2600
$20 for individuals; $10 for nonprofit organizations

International Bottled Water Association
William Deal, Executive Vice President
113 North Henry St.
Alexandria, VA 22314
(703) 683-5213

Chapter 11

Taking Action in Your Community

T he era of unquestioning use of toxic chemicals, promoted by slogans such as "A Better World Through Chemistry," is finished. But it is nearly impossible to undo the harm caused by past disposal of chemicals in a watershed or the discharge of toxic wastes into an unlined landfill. Chemicals mix and disperse in nature so that even a small amount of toxic material creates a large amount of contaminated air, soil, or water. Although we cannot erase past pollution from our environment, we can take immediate action to protect the watershed area of our water supply in the present and for the future.

PUBLIC WATER SUPPLY

Increasingly we read about the hazard of even minute concentrations of a very toxic chemical. The once widely used soil and food fumigant ethylene dibromide or EDB, for example, is hazardous at so tiny an amount as one part per billion (1 ppb). How minute is this infinitesimal quantity? One ppb is an inch in 16,000 miles, which is, roughly, two-thirds the distance around the world. One ppb is four drops of water in an Olympic-sized swimming pool of 64,000 gallons. Because many toxic substances are toxic in such small quantities, those responsible for providing clean and safe municipal water, and private well owners as well, must be vigilant about safeguarding the quality of drinking water by protecting the watershed and recharge area of water supply. The most effective way to do this is to keep toxic chemicals out of the public and private water supply sources.

Every city and town should have a plan to protect its drinking water supply from spills, leaks, and disposal of toxic chemicals and biological waste. The two simplest measures to take are:

1. Zone industry and the water recharge area so that future industry is not located over a public water supply recharge area.

2. Regulate the toxic materials presently stored, used, and disposed of throughout the city.

Many cities and towns are developing ordinances and bylaws to protect and preserve their existing and future water supplies from contamination. These include a **water supply protection plan** to keep new industry and commercial development that handle toxic chemicals out of the recharge area; a **wastewater by-law** for unsewered housing development in the recharge area; and a town or city-wide **hazardous materials ordinance** to ensure safe handling of toxic materials by all industrial and commercial users; a **policy to reduce road salt**; and a **household hazardous waste pickup program.**

WHAT YOUR COMMUNITY CAN DO

1. Adopt a Water Supply Protection By-law.

A zoning by-law, especially developed to create a water supply district, can establish stringent protective measures that will have the necessary effect of discouraging certain types of industrial/commercial development over a critical natural resource.

The following provisions of a water supply protection by-law have been used by communities with unsewered districts and a mix of industrial/commercial/residential zoning and have been adapted by some communities with sewered districts in New England.

USES PROHIBITED IN WATER SUPPLY DISTRICT

- The manufacture, use, storage, transport, or disposal of hazardous materials as a principal activity, including businesses such as metal plating, machine shop, printing, chemical and biological laboratories, pesticide manufacture, dry cleaners

- Sanitary landfills, septage lagoons, wastewater treatment facility

- Road salt stockpile

- Junkyard, salvage yard, truck terminal with more than five trucks

- Gasoline station, car wash, auto or marine repair, auto body shop

- Underground storage of hazardous materials, oil, and gas

Long Island, New York has forbidden the use of septic system cleaners because the public water supply is an aquifer underlying the island.

2. *Adopt a Wastewater Ordinance.*

The purpose of this ordinance is to protect the public drinking water supply from the effluent or hazardous substances discharged from septic tanks and other on-site sewage disposal systems such as dry wells and cesspools. This ordinance would require septic system owners to have their systems pumped on a regular basis—say every two to three years—and prohibit the use of chemical-based septic system cleaners. The town might offer a rebate to be deducted from property taxes for removal of septage by a licensed hauler.

3. *Adopt a Hazardous Materials Ordinance.*

Zoning changes such as a water supply protection by-law are, as a rule, prospective only. All existing land uses are permitted. Only new and expanded industrial/commercial land uses in the drinking water supply area are controlled by zoning. The purpose of the hazardous materials ordinance is to give health officials a record of all hazardous materials stored within the municipality and the authority to establish safety procedures. Most important for drinking water supplies, this ordinance enables health officials to establish and enforce safety procedures for the storage, transport, and disposal of hazardous chemicals by industries located in the watershed or recharge area of the public water supply.

There are state and federal laws for underground storage tanks and for hazardous materials. This ordinance is meant to complement those laws and to give those most responsible for local drinking water—municipal planners and health officials—authority to protect the water supply.

The basic provisions of such an ordinance are:

1. All industries, offices, and individuals storing hazardous materials greater than an established quantity must register with a municipal authority. Information must include the type of material; age, construction, and location of the storage vessel; history of spills or leaks.

2. Owners or operators of industries storing hazardous materials must maintain a monthly inventory of their products received, stored, used, and disposed.

3. State and federal requirements for above-ground and underground storage of hazardous materials must be complied with. These include safety provisions for new and existing underground and above-ground leaks, such as a schedule of leak detection testing, leak detection systems and secondary containment, impermeable surfaces to hold spills.

4. State and federal procedures for abandoned tanks and leaking tanks must be complied with.

4. Establish a Reduced Road Salt Policy.

Those town and state roads that border wellfields and that cross the watershed of groundwater and surface reservoir supplies merit a special policy on the use of road salt. Town planners must designate salt-sensitive areas and negotiate a salt-reduction program with the town and state highway department. Some public works departments have already reduced the amount of salt and increased the amount of sand to as much as 1:10 salt/sand mixture. Often the change is expensive for a city, requiring the purchase of a calibrated salt spreader. Another important factor in salt reduction on roads is educating town crews to use less salt. The best way to avoid high salt levels is to decrease or eliminate using salt and sodium-containing compounds near wells and to divert runoff containing salt away from well sites.

5. Sponsor Household Hazardous Waste Collection.

The first hazardous waste laws targeted industry, to reform the practice of disposing toxic materials in city landfills or in pits and ponds on industrial property. Today the hazardous waste laws have moved from simply restricting disposal practices to encouraging the recycling and reuse of chemicals where possible in order to minimize the amount of waste generated.

Hazardous waste is not created by industry alone. U.S. households generate more than 2 million tons of hazardous waste each year. This waste is from household products such as used motor oil, old car batteries and car wax, household cleaners, empty spray paint cans, old paint and solvent cleaners, weed killers, and pesticides. Although we will not find the word "hazardous" written on most household products, these products are as hazardous as regulated industrial waste. Rat poison is extremely dangerous to humans; oven cleaner is corrosive; and paint thinner and cleaner is ignitable and toxic. The average household stores from 3 to 10 gallons of hazardous waste. Current statistics indicate that as much as 25 percent of all toxic waste originates in individual households. Most of it goes out with the trash to a landfill or incinerator, down the sink or sewer, or into the woods. A change in our household practices can make a significant difference to the environment!

Cities and towns are now sponsoring annual household hazardous waste collections to keep these toxic wastes out of landfills and ultimately out of aquifers. The municipality contracts with a licensed waste hauler and notifies people through the local paper. Here is a sample notice for such a program:

❏ ❏ ❏

HOUSEHOLD HAZARDOUS WASTE PICKUP

Residents of the city of Dover may deposit household hazardous wastes from 9:30 A.M. to 2 P.M., November 19 at the Public Works Department, 209 Wells St., Dover. Persons dropping off materials must be able to prove residency in Dover.

The following categories of waste may be deposited: drain cleaners, cleaning fluids, batteries, pharmaceuticals, photo chemicals, dry cleaning fluids, radiator flushings, wood strippers, oil-based paints, paint thinners, degreasers, asbestos, antifreeze, brake fluids, motor oil, transmission fluids, polishes, pesticides, aerosol insect sprays, rodent poisons, pool chemicals, no-pest strips, and car batteries.

The town will not accept the following materials:

radioactive or explosive materials, ammunition, dioxin, water-reactive materials, lithium batteries, tires, and gas cylinders.

No commercial, industrial, or agricultural wastes will be accepted. Participants should securely package and label the material in its original container, if possible. A chemist may analyze any unlabeled containers, but any unidentified substances may be refused.

For more information, call the Department of Public Works.

❏ ❏ ❏

Toxic waste comes from toxic products. One simple way to reduce toxic waste and protect the environment and drinking water from these wastes is to substitute safe, natural, inexpensive products for hazardous products. A mix of one part lemon to two parts vegetable or olive oil makes a furniture polish, for example. Similar ecological "recipes" for house products, including oven cleaner, window washer, drain cleaner, and all-purpose cleaners, have been developed by environmental groups. The Resources section contains a list of agencies and organizations with information on nonhazardous substitutes for hazardous household products and proper methods of disposal and recycling.

| **WHAT YOU CAN DO** |

Protect Your Private Wells.

Increasingly, private wells are being contaminated by human activities and changes in land use: pesticides on lawns and gardens, septic system cleaners, road salt, cluster housing, and residential housing on former farm and orchard land with pesticide residues. Here are some recommendations for owners of private wells to ensure safer drinking water.

1. **Locate septic systems and animal lots downhill and as far away as possible from the well.** They are a source of nitrate pollution. So also are nitrogen fertilizers, which should be used sparingly.

2. **Pump your septic system every two to three years** to control bacterial contamination. Septic systems and manure are a source of bacterial pollution. Diseases such as typhoid fever, hepatitis, diarrhea, and dysentery can result from sewage contamination of drinking water.

3. **Do not use chemical septic cleaners.** They contain toxic chemicals like methylene chloride and 1,1,1-trichloroethane. These chemicals can kill bacteria important to sewage decomposition in the septic system.

4. **Never pour chemicals such as waste oil and gasoline, paint thinner, furniture remover, disinfectants, and pesticides into drains or into your soil.** To avoid introducing hazardous chemicals into the water supply, minimize your use of them. Most of these products can be identified by reading the labels carefully. Try to substitute less toxic products. If you must use them, cover and store them carefully.

5. **Test your drinking water for pesticides formerly used on your property or if there are any orchards, farms, or rights-of-way nearby your well.** Unlike most other toxic chemicals that are used in a controlled manner, pesticides

are sprayed on the ground, drift on wind, and dissolve or are carried with rain water into the soil. Their use out of doors directly on soil and plants, as well as their toxicity, makes them more hazardous than most other chemicals used.

6. **Encourage your community to sponsor an annual household hazardous waste pickup day.**

Above all, we have to practice locally what we want others to do globally. If we expect farmers and fruit growers to provide us with safe, uncontaminated vegetables and fruit, we must tend our lawns, gardens, and houseplants without contaminating local air, soil, and groundwater. If we look to the federal government to protect national drinking water supplies from increasing contamination, we must also look to our local community to identify and protect local aquifers. If we want industry to minimize hazardous waste and to substitute nontoxic, biodegradable products for toxic ones, should we not do the same in our homes and offices?

RESOURCES

Guides to Action/Organizations
Household Hazardous Waste and Products

Clean Up Your Act (1989)
Public Relations
New England Aquarium
Central Wharf
Boston MA 02110
Free (include a stamped, self-addressed envelope)

How to Run a Household Hazardous Waste Collection Day
Connecticut Department of Environmental Protection
Information and Education Dept.
State Office Building
Hartford, CN 06106
(203) 566-3489
Free

Community Right to Know

State, federal, and many city laws require industries and users of toxic chemicals, except pesticides, to file lists of chemicals and emergency plans with the respective agencies. This public information is a source of information about hazardous chemicals used in your community.

EPA Emergency Planning and Community Right-to-Know Hotline
(800) 535-0202

Using Community Right-to-Know: A Guide to a New Federal Law (1988)
OMB Watch
2001 O St. NW
Washington, DC 20036
(202) 659-1711
$5 for individuals; $25 for national groups

Drinking Water—A Community Action Guide (1986)
Groundwater—A Community Action Guide (1984)
Concern, Inc.
1794 Columbia Road NW
Washington, DC 20009
(202) 328-8160
$3 each

Safety on Tap: A Citizen's Drinking Water Handbook (1987)
David Gray Loveland and Beth Reichheld
League of Women Voters of the United States
1730 M St. NW
Washington, DC 20036
(202) 347-3403
$7.95 for nonmembers

Water Supply Protection By-laws

Model Ordinances for Groundwater Protection
Rural New England, Inc.
P.O. Box 764
Wakefield, RI 02880
(617) 277-4399

Right of Way Vegetation Management Program
Massachusetts Department of Food and Agriculture
Pesticide Bureau
100 Cambridge St.
Boston, MA 02203
(617) 727-7712

Alternative Products

Become an Environmental Shopper (1988)
Pennsylvania Roadside Council
44 East Front St.
Media, PA 19063
(215) 565-9131
Free

Seventh Generation (Catalogue of products for a healthy planet)
10 Farrell Street
South Burlington, Vermont 05403
(802) 862-2999
$2

Reading/Information

Household Hazardous Waste: Conference Summary 1988
Tufts University
Center for Environmental Management
Curtis Hall
474 Boston Ave.
Medford, MA 02155
(617) 381-3486
$22

Household Hazardous Waste Management Newsletter
Waste Watch Center, Inc.
Dana Duxbury and Associates
Corporate Office Centers
16 Haverill St.
Andover MA 01010
(508) 470-3044
Free

PART FOUR

The Ozone Layer: Earth's Evanescent Membrane

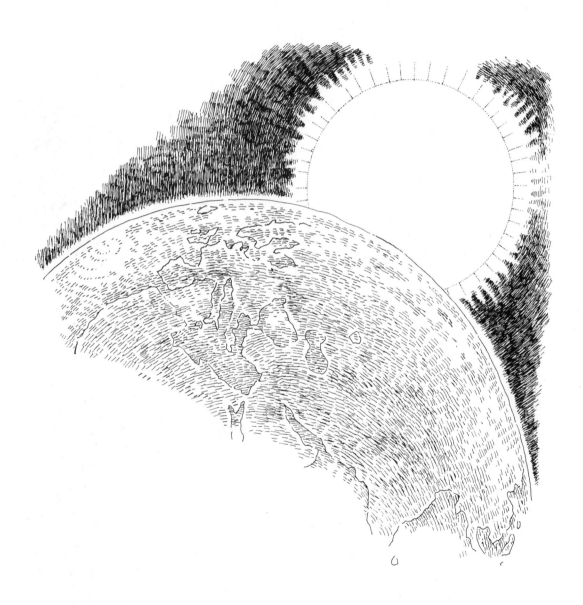

As in a quiet backwater, pollution collects in the stratosphere and no rain washes it away.

Louise Young, *Earth's Aura* (1977)

The vast, invisible sea of air that envelops Earth has molecules of two oxygen atoms bound together and also a minute quantity of *ozone*, that rare form of oxygen in which three oxygen atoms are joined together. Most of the atmospheric ozone is concentrated not in the lower atmosphere where we breathe but some 7 to 15 miles above the Earth's surface in a layer of the upper atmosphere or stratosphere called the ozonosphere or the ozone layer. Ozone is created in the ozonosphere when ultraviolet radiation splits molecules of two-atom oxygen into single atoms, which then recombine with other molecules of two-atom oxygen to produce three-atom ozone. Most of the upper atmosphere ozone is formed where sunlight is strongest—over the tropics—and is circulated by global air patterns toward the North and South Poles. Ozone is destroyed and replenished by natural atmospheric chemistry in a dynamic and fairly stable balance. An average of only a few parts per million ozone has supported the evolution of life on land over millions of years.

Oxygen-breathing life, such as ourselves, could not survive in the thin upper atmosphere of the ozonosphere, but the ozone layer is, nonetheless, critical to Earth's life-support systems. Ozone is the only gas in the atmosphere that screens out much of the most harmful wavelengths of ultraviolet radiation from the sun by absorbing and converting that radiation to heat and chemical energy. The ozone layer—imagined poetically as a planetary umbrella, an invisible shield, and a diffuse, outer membrane that forms part of "Earth's aura"—functions, then, as our planet's natural sunscreen.

In the early 1970s, the invention of a sensitive instrument by Professor James Lovelock—the electron capture detector for gas chromatography—enabled chemists to detect minute quantities of trace chemicals in the upper atmosphere. They soon hypothesized that a chemical component of aerosol sprays was capable of destroying upper atmospheric ozone. Environmental scientists began warning that a gradual thinning of the ozone layer, through destruction of atmospheric ozone molecules, would allow more ultraviolet B (UV-B) radiation (the more biologically damaging bands of ultraviolet radiation) to reach the Earth's surface.

Ultraviolet B rays damage DNA and cause genetic defects, and they have been linked to weakened disease-fighting immune systems in humans and animals. Research shows that UV-B radiation can damage crops and floating fish eggs and larvae for which sunlight is essential, as well as phytoplankton, the microscopic plants that form the basis of the ocean food chain. Plankton begin the vast web of marine life that includes plankton-eating fishes like the herring, the fish-eating fishes like bluefish, the pelagic squid, and the great whale (which may feast on fish, shrimp, or plankton). The tropical seas contain far fewer of these microscopic organisms than the oceans of higher latitudes, in part because there is more ultraviolet radiation at these latitudes.

Tanned, leathered, and wrinkled skin are all caused by ultraviolet radiation. Loss in atmospheric ozone will cause an increase in skin cancer in light-skinned people and more cataracts in eyes. Dermatologists have already documented a great increase in melanoma, a type of skin cancer that can be fatal if not treated. They assess that for every decrease of 1 percent in the ozone layer there is a 2 percent increase in the incidence of skin cancer. The 1989 annual meeting of the American Academy of Dermatology reported that dermatologists are commonly seeing younger people with skin cancer when only a few years ago melanoma was considered a disease of the elderly. Melanoma is now diagnosed at the rate of 1 in 128 Americans, an increase of about 1,500 percent since 1935, reports Dr. Darrell S. Rigel, an assistant clinical professor of dermatology at New York University Medical School. The rate of increase is highest among the youngest people, both in the United States and in other countries, leading dermatologists to suspect, in part at least, the loss in atmospheric ozone. The U.S. Environmental Protection Agency predicts that more than 150 million additional U.S.

people will get skin cancer over the next eighty years if nothing is done to save the thinning ozone layer.

Using computer models, scientists calculate that erosion of the ozone layer at current rates could result in 5 to 20 percent more ultraviolet radiation—most of it in the UV-B band—reaching populated areas within the next forty years. The consequences of doing nothing to halt and reverse this trend threaten terrestrial and aquatic ecosystems and human health. Destruction of the ozone layer is also interrelated with other global ecocrises. The same chemicals that react with and deplete atmospheric ozone have strong heat-absorbing properties. Released to the atmosphere as gases, they are a significant contributor to the greenhouse effect and global warming, accounting for 15 to 20 percent of the projected warming. Second, depletion of the ozone layer can exacerbate local air pollution. Even though stratospheric ozone is vital for life on Earth, at ground level ozone is a dangerous pollutant. In other words, whether ozone is beneficial or harmful hinges on where it is. The main component of smog, ground-level ozone retards crop and tree growth, limits visibility, and damages lung functions. Destruction of the upper ozone layer could increase the amount of ground-level ozone because increased ultraviolet radiation will accelerate the photochemical process that creates smog.

Both the formation of a unique layer of ozone in Earth's upper atmosphere, which enabled life to emerge from the sea onto land, and the atmospheric dynamics that continuously replenish life-sustaining levels of ozone are jeopardized by a few, abundantly used ozone-destroying chemicals. This recent and rapid undoing of ancient, beneficent chemistry, coupled with global warming, may constitute Earth's nemesis.

A few years ago, when depletion of the ozone layer was placed well beyond speculation and dispute onto the firm ground of scientific fact, Secretary of Interior Donald Hodel suggested that we wear sunglasses, hats, and suntan lotion to cope with the hazard of increased ultraviolet radiation. This trivializing of a global problem was ludicrous even then, and it was widely satirized. Today such a reply would be scandalous, so quickly has the entire industrial and developing world been shocked by images of "holes" in the ozone layer over Antarctica. Suddenly, governments are stepping back from protectionist policies toward domestic industries and industrial development; they are holding dramatic international summits and making agreements on limiting the use of the culprit chemicals. But these agreements are outdated before the ink dries as news breaks of worsening ozone depletion. Two simultaneous and connected environmental crises—destruction of the ozone layer and global warming—have galvanized governments worldwide as no crisis related to nuclear power or toxic chemicals has been able to do.

Is the loss of our protective ozone layer inevitable? Can the vanishing ozone layer be recovered? Must we stand by and wait for international agreements among governments, or can we take action now to halt and reverse this trend?

The Worldwatch Institute asserts that current available technologies and stricter standards governing equipment operation and maintenance could reduce the emissions of ozone-depleting chemicals by 90 percent. This material possibility, and also the growing climate of universal urgency and cooperation, compel us to act now at home, at work, and in our communities to help save Earth's evanescent membrane.

Chapter **12**

Not a Better World Through Chemistry

*I*n the late 1920s, the Du Pont Company and the Frigidaire Division of General Motors jointly developed a chemical to be used for heat transfer in the newly introduced refrigerators that were replacing ice boxes. The refrigerant chemical, called chlorofluorocarbons (or CFCs), was nontoxic to humans, nonflammable, and stable—an excellent mix of qualities for domestic use. To demonstrate their relative safety at ground level, Thomas Midgeley, Jr., the research chemist who synthesized CFCs, inhaled vapors from a beaker of clear liquid and then exhaled to extinguish a candle. Du Pont marketed the compound under the trademark Freon. In time, CFCs were used as a refrigerant in home, car, and commercial air conditioners; as a propellant in aerosol spray cans ranging from hairspray and deodorant to furniture polish; as a cleaning solvent by the electronics industry to remove glue, grease, and soldering residues on computer chips; as a sterilant for medical devices; in "high-efficiency" foam insulation; and as an agent to puff up styrofoam products. From manufacture to use, CFCs mushroomed into a multibillion dollar business. If one family of chemicals had been elected to embody the slogan "A Better World Through Chemistry," it would have been chlorofluorocarbons.

Between 1974 and 1988, atmospheric chemists built an unassailable case for the fact that certain widely used CFCs, highly stable in the lower atmosphere, migrate to the upper atmosphere, where they react with and destroy ozone. Another family of chemicals, halons, and two organic solvents, methyl chloroform and carbon

Table 12.1 Global CFC Use, by Category, 1985

Use	Share of Total (percent)
Aerosols	25
Rigid-foam insulation	19
Solvents	19
Air conditioning	12
Refrigerants	8
Flexible foam	7
Other	10

SOURCE: Cynthia Pollock Shea, *Protecting Life on Earth: Steps to Save the Ozone Layer*, Worldwatch Paper 87, Worldwatch Institute, Washington, D.C., December 1988.

tetrachloride, were also identified as major ozone-destroying chemicals. But CFCs are, by far, the most egregious culprit. In the thirteen or so years that a handful of scientists have worked to identify the mechanisms of ozone destruction, the markets for CFCs and other ozone-depleting chemicals expanded as new uses were developed and as developing countries industrialized. For example, following the energy crisis of the 1970s, industrial, commercial, and residential customers used CFC-based rigid-foam insulation in greatly increased quantities. By 1985, rigid-foam insulation accounted for two-thirds of the insulation installed in new U.S. commercial buildings, half the insulation in new single homes, and one-third of the home reinsulation market. Today the foam walls of a household refrigerator contain five times as many CFCs as are used for the refrigerant, a consequence of appliance manufacturers meeting required energy efficiency standards. Table 12.1 provides a profile of worldwide use of CFCs.

The major use of CFCs is in aerosols marketed mainly outside the United States, where they were banned in 1978 as their role in depleting the ozone layer became clear. Rigid-foam insulation and solvent uses in electronics are the fastest growing applications of CFCs. The growth in CFC use has been so great that, despite the ban on CFC aerosols, the United States still has the highest per capita use of ozone-depleting CFCs in the world. European and

Table 12.2 Use and Emissions Profile of Ozone-Depleting Chemicals, 1985

Chemical	Emissions (thousand tons)	Atmospheric lifetime[1] (years)	Applications	Annual growth rate (percent)	Share of contribution to depletion[2] (percent)
CFC-12	412	139	Air conditioning, refrigeration, aerosols, foams	5	45
CFC-11	238	76	Foams, aerosols, refrigeration	5	26
CFC-113	138	92	Solvents	10	12
Carbon tetrachloride	66	67	Solvents	1	8
Methyl chloroform	474	8	Solvents	7	5
Halon 1301	3	101	Fire extinguishers	n.a.	4
Halon 1211	3	12	Fire extinguishers	23	1

[1]Time it takes for 63 percent of the chemical to be washed out of the atmosphere.
[2]Total does not add to 100 due to rounding.

SOURCE: Cynthia Pollock Shea, *Protecting Life on Earth: Steps to Save the Ozone Layer*, Worldwatch Paper 87, Worldwatch Institute, Washington, D.C., December 1988.

Japanese per capita use is not far behind: about 25 percent less per person.

Table 12.2 lists commonly used chemicals that have the highest ozone-depleting potential: three chlorofluorocarbon compounds, two halon compounds, and two organic solvents. Together, Tables 12.1 and 12.2 show at a glance the chemicals and chemical products we use that destroy atmospheric ozone.

Refrigerants in air conditioners and refrigeration account for the highest single U.S. use of CFCs; aerosols account for the highest single European use; and solvents, primarily for the electronics industry, constitute the major single Japanese use. Consumption rates are much less in the rest of the world; a U.S. person consumes six times the global average of CFCs per person. Currently, the third world accounts for 16 percent of the global CFC consumption, but consumption is projected to rise as the industrial base expands.

Halons, compounds that contain bromine, are another family of chemicals that are inert at ground level but long-lived. They are even more reactive with atmospheric ozone than CFCs. Halons were developed by the U.S. Army Corps for fighting fires in tanks during World War II. Now they are used in hand-held fire extinguishers and total-flooding systems for computer rooms, museums, telephone exchanges, and bank storage vaults. Demand for halon fire extinguishers is growing at a rate of 20 to 25 percent annually.

Methyl chloroform and carbon tetrachloride are less publicized ozone-destroying chemicals. Together, however, they contributed 13 percent of total ozone-depleting chemical emissions in 1985, as Table 12.2 shows. Methyl chloroform is used widely as a solvent, especially for metal cleaning; carbon tetrachloride is used to manufacture CFCs and also as a solvent, primarily in Eastern Europe and developing countries. Unlike CFCs and halons, these two chemicals are not regulated under current international treaties. As the use of regulated chemicals diminishes, warns the Worldwatch Institute, use of these two chemicals will grow unless they are brought under regulation.

HOW IS THE OZONE LAYER DESTROYED?

The first suspicions that CFCs migrate to the upper atmosphere and destroy ozone surfaced in the early 1970s. In 1974, an article in a major scientific journal suggested that CFCs, although very stable in the lower atmosphere, decompose in the upper atmosphere and release chlorine atoms that cause ozone molecules to break apart. By 1978, after much pressure from environmental groups, the United States banned CFCs in aerosol cans. At that time, aerosols constituted about half of the total CFC market in the United

States. Canada, Norway, and Sweden also banned CFC propellants in at least 90 percent of their aerosol products; most other countries, however, did not adopt a comparable ban. By the mid-1980s, the international markets for refrigeration, cleaning agents, and foam insulation had grown so that they offset the decline in CFC use from the ban on aerosol sprays. The uses of CFCs were growing globally and would increase drastically in the 1990s.

The 1978 ban on CFC propellants in aerosols, though not ultimately diminishing the production and sales of CFCs, did blunt concern about depletion of the ozone layer, except in a few atmospheric chemists and environmentalists. In early 1985, two British scientists documented an "ozone hole" over Antarctica. This hole, they reported, had been occurring over the South Pole every spring since 1979, as the ozone layer was increasingly thinning. In 1987, virtually all the ozone disappeared in the heart of the ozone layer over Antarctica. The average ozone levels over the entire South Pole plummeted 50 percent. Was this shocking phenomenon peculiar to Antarctica and primarily seasonal?

In March 1988, an international panel of scientists assembled by the National Aeronautics and Space Administration (NASA) reported that the ozone layer is eroding around the entire globe, not only over the south polar region. Further, the erosion was occurring at two to three times the rate that had been predicted. How much and where the erosion was occurring varied with latitude and season. Between 1969 and 1986, the most heavily populated regions of the northern latitudes—Europe, the United States, and the Soviet Union—suffered a year-round depletion of 3 percent and a winter loss of 4.7 percent of atmospheric ozone.

In early 1989, atmospheric scientists found the same chlorine and bromine chemistry in the ozone layer over the North Pole that occurs over Antarctica. That Arctic expedition helped refine our understanding of polar cloud chemistry and how a chlorine-based molecule released from a leaking car air conditioner or vented from a refrigerator by a repairperson, for example, destroys ozone over the poles.

CFCs and halons ascend to the stratosphere, where sunlight breaks them into compounds that are carried northward toward the North Pole by swirling winds. The chemicals attach to crystalline clouds that form over the pole and are held in a slow-moving vortex that forms in the polar winter and breaks up in the spring. Polar stratospheric ice clouds create ideal conditions for ozone destruction by CFCs and halons. In the frigid dark of polar winters, clouds capture and remove nitrogen compounds that would otherwise impede ozone destruction. With the return of sunlight in spring, the chlorine and bromine molecules react rapidly with ozone, each molecule capable of breaking apart hundreds of thousands of ozone molecules.

Figure 12.1, a NASA photograph, taken during the Antarctic spring of 1986, shows the ozone hole over Antarctica. The lightest area in the center—most of it being above the land mass of Antarctica—is the region of very low total ozone, an area about the size of the United States.

The Nimbus 7 satellite has scanned the entire Earth daily since 1979, reading the concentration of total ozone in the stratosphere. These space readings are then reproduced by NASA on photographs showing total ozone distribution in the Northern and Southern Hemispheres. The photographs I viewed portray a small planet Earth finely etched with continents and overlayed with artistic bands of color that represent regional concentrations of ozone. The swatches of color change and mix from photograph to photograph like a cosmic kaleidoscope. Strangely and sadly, these otherwise compelling collages of planet, continent, and shifting color spectra, generated from Nimbus 7 data, reveal the shocking loss of stratospheric ozone between 1979 and 1988.

The March 1979 photo of the Northern Hemisphere shows that the area of lowest ozone, a region bounded in a thin blue band, occurred at mid-latitudes. The March 1987 photo reveals that the blue band has thickened over the mid-latitudes of the Northern Hemisphere, graphically illustrating the loss of ozone over the northern latitudes reported by NASA in the *Global Ozone Trends Report*. The October 1979 plot of the Southern Hemisphere shows the formation of an ozone hole over Antarctica. The Southern Hemisphere photo of total ozone for October 1987 reveals an ozone hole greatly increased in area, nearly as large as the continent of Antarctica. At its center is a dark-hued region representing the lowest ozone value ever observed.

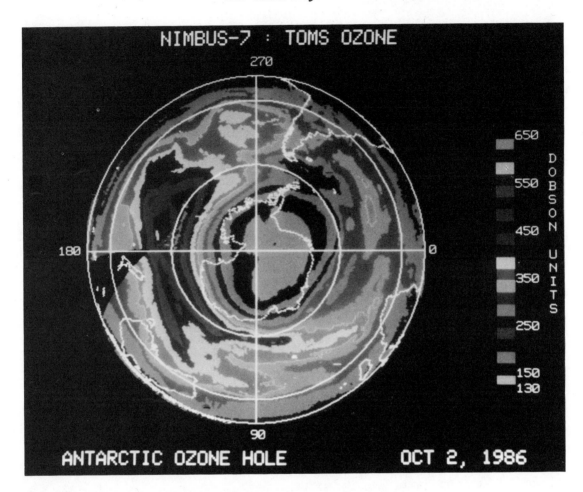

Figure 12.1 The "Ozone Hole" over Antarctica

SOURCE: National Aeronautics and Space Administration, Washington, D.C., October 1986.

Within the last year a world consensus has jelled that those chlorofluorocarbons and halons listed in Table 12.2 are a major cause of these critical changes in stratospheric ozone. CFCs and halons are released or leak into the air when they are manufactured, used, and disposed. Some products, such as aerosols and

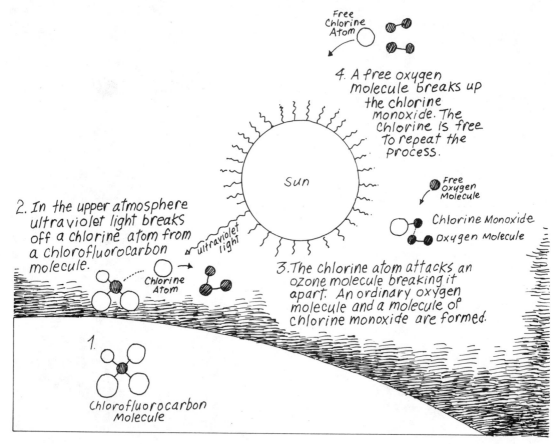

Figure 12.2 How Atmospheric Ozone Is Destroyed

SOURCE: *Protecting the Ozone Layer: What You Can Do* (New York: Environmental Defense Fund, 1988).

solvents, emit CFCs immediately; others, like rigid urethane foams, trap CFC gases inside small holes, where they remain intact for decades until the foam is destroyed or disposed. Because they are very stable, CFCs remain in the atmosphere for decades, moving upward into the lower atmosphere, where they trap heat as "greenhouse" gases, and continuing farther upward to the upper atmosphere. In the stratosphere, CFCs and halons react with ultraviolet light. CFCs lose a chlorine atom; halons lose a bromine atom. These released atoms react with the three-atom ozone to split it apart, as Figure 12.2 shows. One chlorine atom can destroy as many as 100,000 ozone molecules before it becomes inactive or is removed from the atmosphere. Bromine is much more aggressive against ozone than chlorine.

Even if the entire world were to stop using CFCs and halons immediately, destruction of the ozone layer would go on for decades because the average travel time for a CFC molecule from ground level to the ozone layer ranges from twenty to fifty years. The chlorine will reside in the Ozonosphere many more years. CFCs and halons discharged in the past are still migrating in the atmosphere toward the ozone layer. Those destroying the layer were released decades ago from aerosol cans, defective and abandoned refrigerators and air conditioners, and the testing of fire extinguishing systems. The destruction of the ozone layer over Antarctica from CFCs and halons *used today* will continue into the twenty-first century. The Natural Resources Defense Council estimates that even with an immediate total ban on ozone-depleting chemicals, recovery of the ozone layer will take more than a century.

Other projections, based on realistic expectations of slow government and industry action, are more foreboding. Two million tons of substances containing chlorine and bromine are still on the ground, trapped in insulation foams, appliances, junked automobiles, and fire-fighting equipment. Under the most current optimistic regulatory scenarios, warns the Worldwatch Institute, chlorine concentrations in the upper atmosphere are expected to triple by the year 2075; bromine concentrations will grow considerably faster.

RESOURCES

Reading/Information

Earth's Aura (1977)
Louise Young
Avon Books
New York
$2.95

Environmental Protection Agency
Global Change Division
Washington, DC 20460
(202) 382-7750

Studies on depletion of ozone layer, CFC substitutes, etc.

Global Lessons from the Ozone Hole (1988)
Michael Oppenheimer
Environmental Defense Fund
257 Park Avenue South
New York, NY 10010
(212) 505-2100
$20

Global Ozone Trends Report (March 1988)
National Aeronautics and Space Administration
Washington, DC 20546
(202) 783-5109
Free

Photos in black and white and color of total ozone distribution in Northern and Southern Hemispheres are also available from NASA.

Stones in a Glass House: CFCs and Ozone Depletion (1988)
Douglas G. Cogan
Investor Responsibility Research Center, Inc.
1755 Massachusetts Ave. NW, Suite 600
Washington, DC 20036
(202) 939-6500
$30

Chapter 13

What Can Be Done?

If companies don't reclaim the CFCs in their equipment, they are doing to the atmosphere what Exxon did to the Arctic.

Carmelo J. Scuderi, chief engineer, ThermaFlo

*I*n September 1987, after years of arduous and heated negotiation, the United States and twenty-three nations signed an international ozone agreement, called the Montreal Protocol, to freeze CFC production at 1986 levels and to reduce CFC production in industrial countries by 50 percent and freeze halon production by 1998. Governments and government environmental agencies rarely move drastically; consequently, they proclaimed the Montreal Protocol to be a major step in global action.

Less than a month after the Protocol was signed, the largest hole ever detected in the ozone layer over Antarctica was recorded by the Nimbus 7 satellite. In spring 1988, NASA released the *Global Ozone Trends Report*, revealing that the global ozone layer is eroding all over the globe, not just in polar regions as it was commonly alleged. The report revealed that the world had already suffered more ozone loss than the Montreal Protocol had anticipated would occur by the year 2050.

Environmentalists who work on atmospheric pollution were already convinced that the phaseout of CFCs in the Montreal Protocol was too little and would be too late. With cuts in CFCs of only 50 percent by 1998, the ozone layer would steadily deteriorate. The *Global Ozone Trends Report* confirmed this projection, thereby rendering the goals of the Montreal Protocol obsolete.

Certain industrial and industrializing countries have reacted to the new bad news by moving up the target dates on reduction of CFC use. In late February 1989, the twelve nations of the European Community vowed to eliminate production of the most harmful CFCs by the end of the century. President Bush has proposed an international agreement to accomplish the same goal. In May

1989, eighty nations met under U.N. sponsorship in Helsinki to adopt a declaration that agrees to phase out the chemicals controlled by the Montreal Protocol as soon as possible, but not later than the year 2000. At this same meeting, some countries called for the inclusion of other ozone-depleting chemicals, such as halon gases, methyl chloroform, and carbon tetrachloride. So far, though, all these actions are only theoretical endorsements of phaseouts, and even the new endorsements do not go far enough.

Sweden is the first country to move beyond paper endorsements and to accelerate the schedule of eliminating the use of chlorofluorocarbons. In June 1988, the Swedish parliament passed legislation that eliminates CFCs in that country by 1995. After extensive discussions with industry, the government established a schedule of phasing out sterilant and remaining aerosol uses of CFCs by the end of 1988; use in packaging by the end of 1989; use as a solvent and in flexible foam by 1991; use in rigid foam, in dry-cleaning, and as coolants by 1994 at the latest. If it becomes possible to phase out any uses earlier than the deadlines, Swedish industries are obliged to do so. Sweden represents only 1 percent of CFC use worldwide, so it is imperative that other countries, especially large users, follow that country's stellar example.

The United States is the single largest contributor to ozone depletion, generating 30 percent of worldwide emissions of ozone-depleting chemicals. Environmentalists are calling for the Environmental Protection Agency to propose regulations to phase out completely by mid-1990 the manufacture of ozone-depleting CFCs and to put in place immediate recycling and reuse programs for currently used CFCs. In late 1988, the EPA also concluded that reduction to 50 percent by 1998, as the Montreal Protocol calls for, would not stabilize the amount of ozone-destroying chlorine released from CFCs. The agency called for faster and complete elimination of ozone-depleting chemicals, adding methyl chloroform, the widely used industrial solvent, to the list. Environmental groups asked to see action on this, calling for the United States not to wait for a new international agreement that would revise the Montreal Protocol, but to take unilateral action to phase out 100 percent of all ozone-depleting chemicals.

Everyone—environmentalists, industry, and government—

agrees that it will take several years before alternative chemicals are extensively substituted for CFCs and halons. In the interim, then, we need to limit ongoing emissions *immediately* with state and local recovery and recycling initiatives and to start campaigns to purchase products that do not contain ozone-depleting chemicals. Environmentalists are confident that a high percentage—some quote as high as 90 percent—of emissions of CFCs and halons can be reduced in the short term by recycling CFCs and by using alternative products.

CFC emissions can be drastically reduced by a total ban on CFC propellants in aerosol cans and by recovering CFCs that evaporate from solvents and those that are customarily vented to the atmosphere from refrigeration systems. The recycling program should be coupled with an aggressive five-year plan like that of Sweden: to develop safe replacement chemicals and technologies. Such an ambitious, rapid-fire program will require a concert of government, business, and individual initiative and commitment.

GOVERNMENT ACTION

Congress should not wait for action by the EPA. In 1988, four federal bills were introduced to protect the ozone layer, but none of them was enacted in the 100th Congress. The consensus among environmentalists is that new congressional legislation should contain the following elements:

- Ban production and use of major ozone-depleting CFCs and halons by 1995.

- Ban unnecessary uses and wasteful practices. Require recycling and reuse of ozone-depleting chemicals wherever possible.

- Label products made with ozone-depleting chemicals to warn consumers and to encourage environmentally conscious buying.

● Tax the windfall profits that CFC and halon manufacturers will reap from a phasedown of their use.

● Prohibit imports of products made with ozone-depleting chemicals from countries that refuse to end their use.

WHAT YOU CAN DO

1. Vote Conservation.

The League of Conservation Voters is a bipartisan organization that supports candidates of both political parties on the basis of their environmental records and positions. The League is governed by a board of directors that includes leaders from almost every major environmental organization in the United States. The League has developed a "survival agenda" for the U.S. Congress that is the first general statement of the political actions necessary to preserve the ozone layer, slow global warming, reduce acid rain, and protect oceans and rainforests. As for CFCs, the survival agenda calls for the elimination of their use by the mid-1990s. In the interim, a heavy tax should be placed on their use and strong warning labels should be required on products made with or containing these chemicals. Recycling ozone-depleting chemicals should be mandated by law.

Write your congressperson to support this agenda, and require new candidates to state their position on the environmental survival agenda. The measures won't be popular in Congress by the usual gauge—cost. They will require Americans to change dramatically the way we use energy, dispose of trash, and produce electricity. These solutions will increase the prices we pay for electricity, gasoline, building construction, and CFC-based products. They will mean less packaging for food and consumer products. Adopting the survival agenda will require courageous action on the part of Congress and a few "lifestyle" changes for individuals. Is the global atmosphere not worth at least this?

THE LEAGUE OF CONSERVATION VOTERS' SURVIVAL AGENDA FOR THE U.S. CONGRESS

☐ SLOW GLOBAL WARMING: Achieve at least a 20% reduction on CO2 emission levels by the year 2000 through measures to require greater energy conservation and efficiency under a national energy plan. Use tax incentives, regulatory reform and direct funding to increase the development of renewable energy sources such as wind, solar, biomass and hydrogen cells. Encourage the use of natural gas and increase motor vehicle fuel efficiency standards. Increase funding for family planning services to control world population growth. Establish an Office of Climate Protection in the Energy Department and begin a comprehensive study on the long-term effects and possible ways to adapt to the effects of global warming.

☐ HALT NEW OZONE DEPLETION: Eliminate the usage of CFCs in the next five years. In the interim, place a heavy tax on their use and require strong warning labels on products containing or made with these chemicals. In repairing air conditioners, require the use of "vampires," a machine that recycles chlorofluorocarbons instead of simply releasing these chemicals into the atmosphere.

☐ STOP ACID RAIN: Cut sulfur dioxide emissions by 12 million tons per year and achieve a dramatic reduction in nitrogen oxide emissions through tougher emission standards.

☐ SAVE THE RAINFORESTS: Authorize the establishment of a Multilateral Tropical Forestry and Agroforestry program to seek international cooperation to reduce and halt the destruction of rainforests in the third world. Adopt legislation facilitating the protection of rainforests in exchange for debt forgiveness. Establish common international principles on rainforest protection and ban the import of wood and wood products from nations failing to support these principles.

☐ PROTECT THE OCEANS: Expand enforcement provisions of the Clean Water Act to speed compliance with the "no discharge" goals of the Clean Water Act. Outlaw the export of hazardous waste to developing nations and ban ocean dumping.

SOURCE: The League of Conservation Voters, Washington, D.C., 1989.

2. Demand Action from the Executive Branch.

Under the Clean Air Act, the Environmental Protection Agency has the responsibility to control U.S. production and use of ozone-depleting chemicals. The Clean Air Act also directs the President to negotiate international agreements, with the assistance of EPA and the State Department, to control these chemicals worldwide. Write President Bush and insist that the United States negotiate an international agreement to phase out CFCs and halons by 1995. Write the EPA administrator, William Reilly, and demand that he support the agreement. Demand that he undertake the following five-part program, as developed by the Natural Resources Defense Council (shown in the box on page 157).

3. Support State and Local Legislation.

In May 1989, the state of Vermont curbed the use of CFCs with the strictest law yet passed in the United States. The law requires that, beginning in 1993, automobiles and other vehicles air conditioned by CFCs will be banned from registration and sale in Vermont. This action, called "foolish" and "unattainable" by the auto trade association, matches the strictest action taken in the world to date: a total ban, by 1994, of all forms of CFC production in Sweden. Volvo told the Vermont bill sponsor that it expects to adapt its air conditioners in time to meet the deadline of the Swedish bill.

How "foolish" and "unattainable" is the Vermont state law? In October 1989, Rovac Auto Air Condition Systems demonstrated an auto air conditioner with a rotary compressor that can use refrigerants that are alternatives to CFC-12, the ozone-depleting CFC currently used. The demonstration took place in Washington, D.C. at an international conference on chlorofluorocarbon and halon substitutes sponsored by the EPA and the Alliance for Responsible CFC Policy. At this same conference, General Motors announced its goal of replacing CFC-12 (commonly called R-12) in air conditioners with an alternative chemical by 1994 model year.

Mobile air conditioners emit more than three times as much CFC gas as do home and commercial refrigerators. Although the gas is sealed in cooling units, many mobile units lose R-12 from

SAVING THE OZONE LAYER:
CONTACT THE FEDERAL GOVERNMENT

Write President Bush. Remind him of his campaign promise to phase out CFCs and other ozone-depleting chemicals. Tell him protecting the ozone layer should be one of his highest domestic and foreign policy priorities. Ask him to direct his Secretary of State to reach a new international agreement *this year* to phase out CFCs and halons by 1995. Ask him to order his EPA Administrator to issue new rules to eliminate U.S. emissions.

> President George Bush
> 1600 Pennsylvania Avenue, N.W.
> Washington, D.C. 20500

Write the EPA Administrator. Demand action to carry out the President's call for a total world-wide phase-out of CFCs and halons. Tell him you support the effort to obtain a stronger international treaty. But tell him to clean up our own house too. Demand that he undertake the following five-part phase-out program:

• Issue new regulations to phase out U.S. production and use of CFCs and halons by 1995;

• Make early emission reductions by immediately ending unnecessary uses and wasteful practices;

• Require labels on products made with CFCs or halons to warn consumers of the danger to the ozone layer;

• Charge a fee on CFCs and halons to recoup the estimated $2.7 billion windfall profit that producers will reap from a phase-down;

• Ban imports of products made with CFCs and halons from countries that refuse to adopt equivalent phase-out rules.

> William Reilly, Administrator
> Environmental Protection Agency
> 401 M Street, S.W.
> Washington, D.C. 20480

SOURCE: *Saving the Ozone Layer: A Citizen Action Guide* (New York: Natural Resources Defense Council, 1988).

vibration and during repair. The Vermont law will require that repair shops use equipment to recapture and recycle the refrigerant gas, a requirement being considered by many other state legislatures. **Support legislation in your state to accelerate the sale of new auto air conditioners that do not use R-12 and to require that auto repair shops immediately begin to recycle R-12.**

INDUSTRY ACTION

The family of chlorofluorocarbons (CFCs) contains many chemical compounds. Three of these, known as CFC-11, CFC-12, and CFC-113, are the major ozone destroyers. These three compounds comprise 90 percent of CFC manufacture in the United States. The Du Pont Company, which originally developed the chlorofluorocarbons and has manufactured about one quarter of the world's annual production of 2 billion pounds of chlorofluorocarbons, announced in March 1988 that it would phase out production of these three compounds by the end of the century. These same three compounds are the subject of the Montreal Protocol.

As refrigerants alone, CFC-11 and CFC-12 are used in 100 million home refrigerators, in the air conditioners of 90 million cars, and in the central air conditioning plants of 100,000 large buildings in the United States. What are the alternatives? The primary ozone-destroying refrigerant, CFC-12, could be replaced with HFC-134a. Chemical engineers say that the chemical is more difficult to manufacture, will be more costly than CFC-12, and may need to be replaced more often. It cannot be used in refrigeration equipment previously operated with CFC-12. In September 1988, Du Pont announced that it would begin commercial production of HFC-134a in 1990 at Corpus Christi, Texas. This significant step in replacing CFC-12 in auto air conditioners, home and commercial refrigerators and freezers, and chillers for large building air conditioners represents 40 percent of the U.S. CFC market. The proposed replacement for CFC-11, used to make plastic foam and as a refrigerant in central air conditioning systems, is HCFC-22, a compound already used in home air conditioners. Not having the heat-insulating characteristics of CFC-11, its applications are more limited.

In March 1989, Du Pont announced that it has developed two potential substitutes for CFC-113, used in solvents for cleaning glue, grease, and soldering residues from electronics components. Equally effective on metals and plastic and even on fabrics, CFC-113 is the fastest growing compound in the CFC group. Prior to this announcement, the American Telephone and Telegraph Company and a small company, Petroferm, Inc., announced the joint development of a new, environmentally safe compound for cleaning electronic circuit boards, superior to CFC-113 and other chlorinated solvents. The new product, BIOACT (registered as EC-7) contains a number of products that can be extracted from natural materials including citrus fruit rinds and wood. Substituting the new compound for CFC-113 requires a new process and new equipment for cleaning the solder off the circuit boards after the integrated electronic circuits have been attached. On August 1, 1989, A.T. & T. announced that it would end all uses of chemicals that deplete the ozone layer by 1994. A.T. & T. uses 3 million pounds of CFC-113 per year, making the company one of the world's largest consumers of CFC compounds. Other major telecommunications companies such as Northern Telecom, Inc. of Canada and Seiko Epson of Japan have made a public commitment to reduce drastically their use of CFCs as a solvent.

The three widely used chlorofluorocarbons have extraordinarily useful properties: low boiling points and high vapor pressures, which make them ideal as refrigerants and propellants in aerosol cans. They are relatively nontoxic at ground level and chemically unreactive, so they do not corrode materials they contact. Under pressure, they wet any material they touch, more so than water, making them excellent for cleaning microscopic pores of circuit boards. Many of the substitutes are less durable, are inferior in industrial properties, and require a redesign of much equipment. They break down more quickly in the lower atmosphere, posing much less threat to the ozone layer. Industry and the EPA warn, however, that they may be more toxic to humans exposed to them than CFCs. One participant at the October 1989 EPA conference on chlorofluorocarbon and halon substitutes raised the question of substitutes causing other climate changes, such as acid rain. The substitution of one set of industrial chemicals that destroy the ozone layer for another set of chemicals that are toxic to humans or potentially harmful to climate is myopic. We want alternatives that are safe.

WHAT YOU CAN DO

1. Put the Pressure on Industry.

In the United States, five companies manufacture CFCs and three companies make halons. Only Du Pont has committed to a more or less specific deadline for ending its production of CFCs by the turn of the century. This is twice as long as environmentalists think the process should take. None of the producers of halons has committed to a phaseout of halons. After years of opposing a phaseout, the industry's trade association, the Alliance for Responsible CFC Policy, recently gave qualified support to ending production of the most dangerous CFCs.

The Natural Resources Defense Council recommends that people put pressure on these companies and the CFC industry trade association to phase out these chemicals and introduce *safe* alternatives by 1994–1995. (See box on pages 161–162.)

2. Exert Consumer Power.

Before the U.S. government banned most uses of CFC aerosol sprays in 1978, many people voluntarily stopped buying them. Between 1974 and 1978, people wrote more letters to Congress on this issue than any other since the Vietnam War. Individual states passed laws banning sale of CFC aerosols or requiring that those products be labeled. Pump sprays and roll-ons started to appear on the market. Sales of CFC-based aerosols dropped in half by the time EPA banned all but "essential" uses of CFC-based propellants.

SAVING THE OZONE LAYER:
CONTACT MAJOR CORPORATIONS

Write the chief executives of these companies. Ask them where they stand. Demand specific commitments to a crash program to phase out CFCs and halons and introduce safe alternatives by 1994.

CFCs:

> Mr. Edgar S. Woolard, Jr., President
> E.I. Du Pont de Nemours & Co., Inc.
> 1007 Market Street
> Wilmington, Delaware 19898

> Mr. Alan Belzer, President
> Allied-Signal Inc.
> Columbia Road & Park Avenue
> P.O. Box 3000R
> Morristown, New Jersey 07960

> Mr. Seymour S. Preston, III, President
> Pennwalt Corporation
> Three Parkway
> Philadelphia, Pennsylvania 19102

> Mr. William LaRoche, President
> LaRoche Chemical, Inc.
> P.O. Box 1031
> Baton Rouge, LA 70821

> Mr. Maurice Knopf, President
> Racon Inc.
> 6040 S. Ridge Road
> P.O. Box 196
> Wichita, Kansas 67201

Halons:

> Mr. Edgar S. Woolard, Jr., President
> E.I. Du Pont de Nemours & Co., Inc.
> (same address as above)

> Mr. Harry Coreless, Chairman
> ICI Americas, Inc.
> Rollins Building, 10th Floor
> Wilmington, Delaware 19897

Mr. Emerson Kampen, President
Great Lakes Chemical Corporation
P.O. Box 2200
West Lafayette, Indiana 47906

The many industries that *use* CFCs and halons also share the responsibility for phasing them out. The chemicals are contained in, or used in the manufacture of, a wide variety of products: refrigerators and air conditioners, automobiles, computers and electronics, foam insulation and packaging, fire extinguishers, and many others. Write to the industry's association of producers and users, the Alliance for Responsible CFC Policy.

Mr. Richard C. Barnett, Chairman
Alliance for Responsible CFC Policy
1901 Ft. Myer Drive
Rosslyn, VA 22209

SOURCE: *Saving the Ozone Layer: A Citizen Action Guide* (New York: Natural Resources Defense Council, 1988).

Consumer action was a potent force then and can be now for many CFC products commonly used in the home, workplace and community. All environmentalists agree that immediate reductions in CFC emissions can be achieved by eliminating evaporation of cleaning solvents; recovering the refrigerants drained from cooling systems being repaired; plugging the leaks in air conditioning and refrigeration systems; banning CFC propellants in aerosols; and using alternative non-CFC products.

a. Limit Polystyrene Foam Products.

Polystyrene foams, with a characteristic bead texture, are used as blowing agents to make styrofoam drinking cups, packaging chips, ice chests, and flotation products. In April 1988, the Food-service and Packaging Institute announced plans to replace CFC-11 and CFC-12 with HCFC-22 in the manufacture of polystyrene foam by early 1989. HCFC-22 has 1/20th the ozone depletion potential of CFC-11 and CFC-12. Although this is a major step, HCFC-22 is still an ozone depleter. Therefore, we feature here initiatives taken by individuals, companies, and communities to limit the use of polystyrene foam products with or without CFCs.

Figure 13.1

The Massachusetts Port Authority discontinued use of styrofoam products at all Massport facilities beginning January 1988. The policy was announced to all employees in a memo from the Chief of Environmental Management that explained the compelling environmental reasons and how to implement the policy.

MASSPORT POLICY REGARDING USE OF DISPOSABLE POLYSTYRENE PRODUCTS AT MASSPORT FACILITIES

January 7, 1988

The discontinuation of use of polystyrene (commonly known as Styrofoam, the Dow Chemical Company trade name) products is proposed at all Massport facilities. There are three compelling environmental reasons for implementing this policy:

1. Such products are non-biodegradable and non-recyclable and therefore contribute to the landfill shortage crisis in Massachusetts and New England.

2. The incineration of polystyrene material causes the emission of toxic air pollutants.

3. The manufacture of such products involves the use of chlorofluorocarbons (CFCs) which are endangering the protective ozone layer so vital to human health, and the productivity of farms, forests and fisheries. CFCs are used in the polystyrene manufacturing processes to inject tiny air bubbles into the product.

It is important that the Massachusetts Port Authority join the many other state and local governments and institutions nationwide in substituting the use of these harmful products with biodegradable paper products.

This policy will be implemented in the following ways:

1. The Massachusetts Port Authority will initiate no new purchases of polystyrene products of any kind and attempts will be made to renegotiate existing contracts in order to substitute paper products for polystyrene materials. Coffee rooms throughout the Authority's Logan, Bridge, Real Estate, Maritime and State Transportation Building offices will be stocked with paper products only. Caterers will be required to comply with the policy when doing Massport business.

The Pro-Environment Packaging Council represents paper companies that manufacture paper goods and paper packaging, using molded pulp and paperboard that can be substituted for foam products. They provide names of alternative packaging products and suppliers.

2. In existing leases where Massport has approval authority over so-called single-service ware selection, only paper products will be approved.

3. All future concessionaire leases will include approval clauses for the above stated purpose.

4. All other tenants will be advised of this policy and encouraged to seek alternative products.

SOURCE: Robin Ellis, Chief of Environmental Management, Massachusetts Port Authority, Boston, 1988.

b. Select non-CFC Insulation.

Certain cities and states have passed ordinances that restrict or ban the use of foam packaging. They include the state of Vermont; the state of Maine; Berkeley, California; Amherst, Massachusetts; and Suffolk County, New York.

Rigid-foam insulation, primarily used in walls, basements, floors, and roofing, contains CFCs that will eventually be released to the atmosphere. Until it is manufactured without CFC-11, consider using alternatives such as fiberglass, fiberboard, gypsum, and foil-laminated board. Air-blown cellulose insulation can be substituted for blown, sprayed, or poured foam insulation. Although its insulation effectiveness per inch is less than that of foam, cellulose can be applied in thicker quantities to achieve the same insulation value.

c. Do Not Buy Halon Home Fire Extinguishers.

Halons are similar in structure to chlorofluorocarbons. Halon fire extinguishers were developed for fighting fires in computers and other valuable electronic and electric systems as well as in museums and libraries where water and other fire-fighting chemicals would destroy valuable items. Most home extinguishers use dry chemicals, but not halons. Halon extinguishers, however, are being marketed increasingly for home use. Although they are currently produced in small quantities, the production of halons is growing. Do not buy halon fire extinguishers for home use; they are not necessary.

The state of Hawaii enacted a law in early 1989 that will take effect in 1991 to prohibit the willful release of CFCs to the atmosphere. The measure bans the over-the-counter sale of refrigerants such as those used in car air conditioning systems. It bans the sale of Freon cartridges used in automobile air conditioning recharge kits and requires professional mechanics to recover and recycle CFCs.

The General Motors Company has developed a comprehensive strategy for the use of CFCs in their auto air conditioners: *Conserve, reclaim*, and *replace*. GM does not test its units with CFCs. CFC recycling is mandated in all serviceships by 1991. By 1994 model year, CFCs will be replaced with an alternative, HFC-134a and all vehicle systems will be modified in new vehicles.

d. Repair Leaky Auto Air Conditioner at Dealer that Recycles CFCs.

The single largest source of CFCs emitted to the atmosphere in the United States is leaky auto air conditioners. CFC-12, also known as R-12, is used in automobile air conditioners to charge units, to service and restock domestic and imported units, and to replace lost test gases during manufacture. When a car air conditioner is serviced, the refrigerant is typically removed by venting to the atmosphere. Recovery equipment is now available, however, that pumps the refrigerant out of the compressor, cleans and purifies the refrigerant for use, and stores or transfers the refrigerant while air conditoners are being repaired.

If your air conditioner is leaking, don't just refill it with over-the-counter cans of CFC refrigerant that will leak more CFCs into the air. Have it repaired to stop emitting CFCs to the atmosphere. If your system shows signs of failing, have it serviced sooner rather than later. Choose a shop carefully: Many treat a leak simply by adding more R-12. Have your air conditioner recharged at a service station with recovery and recycling equipment that drains, cleans, and reuses the CFCs in your auto. Although these recycling units are not yet abundant, states will increasingly require mandatory recycling.

The industry trade association is urging service stations to use a vacuum system rather than pumping up a system with R-12 to find a leak; to keep careful inventories of supplies; and to look for more than one leak before repressurizing the system. They predict that many more service stations will have recycling equipment by 1990 and 1991. The trade association maintains a list of service stations that comply with its recommendations.

Using the motto "You can make a difference," the Mobile Air Conditioning Society (MACS) has taken a lead role in encouraging auto service shops to invest in refrigerant recycling equipment and voluntarily implement refrigerant recycling in their service bays as soon as possible. MACS estimates that a universal recycling program for mobile air conditioners can reduce this largest single source of CFCs by 60 percent. Dr. Stephen Anderson, Chief of the Technology and Economics Branch of the EPA's Division of

---

**NATURAL RESOURCES DEFENSE COUNCIL
STRATOSPHERIC DISTRESS CARD**

Carry this card in your wallet or purse.
Use it to check labels at the store to know which products to avoid.

CFC-11	Trichlorofluoromethane
CFC-12	Dichlorodifluoromethane
CFC-113	Trichlorotrifluoroethane
CFC-114	Dichlorotetrafluoroethane
CFC-115	(Mono)chloropentafluoroethane
Halon-1211	Bromochlorodifluoroethane
Halon-1301	Bromotrifluoroethane
Halon-2402	Dibromotetrafluoroethane

SOURCE: *Saving the Ozone Layer: A Citizen Action Guide* (New York: Natural Resources Defense Council, 1988).

Global Change, adds that use of CFC recycling equipment in automobile air conditioners will provide the "greatest single reduction to date of CFC-12 emissions into the atmosphere."

e. Avoid CFC Aerosols.

The EPA banned nonessential uses of CFCs as an aerosol propellant in 1978. There are some CFC-containing aerosols still sold that you can avoid—for example, spray cans of plastic confetti; aerosol dirt removers for photography equipment; cleaning sprays for sewing machines, VCRs, and electronic equipment. Increasingly, products will be labeled to indicate whether or not they contain the most harmful ozone-depleting chemicals. On this page is a handy reference card prepared by the Natural Resources Defense Council that you can use to check product labels to identify CFC-free products.

f. Old Cars and Appliances Can No Longer Be "Out of Sight, Out of Mind."

In early 1989, I purchased a new refrigerator from Sears, Roebuck and Company. For $25 the company removed the old one. Later I called the local Sears store to track down the fate of my old refrigerator—specifically, the environmental fate of the CFCs in the compressor. "What does Sears do with the CFCs—throw them away with the appliance, vent them, or recycle them?" I asked each service person, manager, and technician I was routed and rerouted to at the regional and then national level. I was able to ascertain that Sears uses a private contractor to dispose of old refrigerators. But no one could tell me if Sears has a companywide policy on recycling CFCs, for repair as well as disposal of refrigerators, that would apply equally to their private disposal contractors. Unable to get my inquiry answered, I wrote the company president (see Figure 13.2).

Sears has not yet answered my letter, although I have been informed that the company is making inquiries about recycling machines. Meanwhile I have undertaken my own research into safe disposal of old appliances that contain CFCs and other hazardous substances and sent this information to Sears in a second letter (see Figure 13.3).

Chlorofluorocarbons are being released slowly from junked automobiles, abandoned refrigerators, and discarded foam insulation in quantities, some analysts estimate, that are equivalent to ten years' worth of current CFC production. The most comprehensive program in the United States for disposing of old appliances in an environmentally sound manner may be one originally set up for a different purpose. Wisconsin Electric Power Company initiated a Smart Money Energy Program to offer its customers rebates for turning in old, operating refrigerators, freezers, and air conditioners in exchange for new, energy-efficient ones. The savings in energy would delay the need for new power plants. During the first two years, more than 92,000 units turned in were shredded at scrap yards to reclaim the metal for reuse. (When refrigerators and air conditioners are shredded, the CFC refrigerant is released to the atmosphere.) The old appliances are now picked up for the power company by a recycling company, Appliance Recycling Centers of America (ARCA), that removes and recycles all chlorofluorocarbons. Any other hazardous substances, such as PCB capacitors in pre-1979 refrigerators, are removed and disposed of as hazard-

I W T

Institute on Women and Technology

P.O. Box 338

North Amherst, Massachusetts 01059

(413) 367-9725

July 26, 1989

Mr. Michael Bozic, President
Sears, Roebuck, and Company
Sears Tower
Chicago, Illinois 60684

Dear Mr. Bozic,

In April I purchased a refrigerator from the Sears, Roebuck and Company store in Dedham, Massachusetts. I also paid Sears $25.00 to remove the old refrigerator. For the past three months, I have called your regional and national offices to find out what Sears does with old refrigerators. My specific concern has to do with the chlorofluorocarbons (CFCs) in the compressor. What is the company policy on CFCs in old refrigerators disposed of by Sears or by a contractor of Sears? No one thus far has been able to tell me.

As you know, CFCs are the chemical most responsible for depletion of the ozone layer. Historically, CFCs have been removed from refrigeration equipment by venting to the atmosphere during repair and at the time of disposal. Technology now exists to remove and filter CFC refrigerants, to store them in any standard receiver, and to charge a system from the receiver. What system of CFC removal for servicing and disposal of appliances does your company use?

Currently, I am writing a guide to environmental action, EarthRight (Prima 1990), which contains a chapter on depletion of the ozone layer. The guide features actions and policies that citizens, communities and companies can take to reduce the use and disposal of ozone-depleting chemicals. One of the recommended actions is to recover CFCs when refrigerators and automobiles are disposed. Sears, Roebuck and Company can take an exemplary role in this action.

I look forward to your reply.

Sincerely,

H. Patricia Hynes
Director

Figure 13.2

I_{W_T} Institute on Women and Technology

P.O. Box 338
North Amherst, Massachusetts 01059
(413) 367-9725

October 15, 1989

Mr. Michael Bozic, President
Sears, Roebuck and Company
Sears Tower
Chicago, Illinois 60684

Dear Mr. Bozic,

I have received no reply to my letter of July 26, 1989 (copy enclosed). Recently, EPA and the Alliance for Responsible CFC Policy held a conference in Washington, DC on CFC and halon substitutes. Also featured at the conference were CFC recycling and reclaiming equipment, some of which is now UL listed. The trade association, Mobile Air Conditioning Society, is encouraging all of its members to install recycling equipment in their service bays voluntarily. General Motors announced a CFC strategy of <u>conserve, recycle, and reclaim</u>, which includes no testing with CFCs and installing recycle/ reclaim equipment in all serviceships by 1991.

I would challenge Sears to take such a lead in the home appliance field for repair and disposal of refrigerator compressors containing CFC refrigerants. I await your response and would like to feature this kind of environmentally responsible initiative in my forthcoming book, <u>EarthRight</u>.

Sincerely,

H. Patricia Hynes
Director

cc. Senator John Kerry

Figure 13.3

ous waste. ARCA rebuilds the appliances that are reusable and sells the ferrous and nonferrous metal to metal recyclers. ARCA provides similar curbside collection and recycling services in St. Paul–Minneapolis, St. Louis, Atlanta, and Milwaukee. Residents in Scott County, Minnesota pay $10 for every appliance they dump at the county landfill. The landfill pays ARCA $6 for each appliance it hauls away. Arca removes CFCs and PCBs; rebuilds and resells appliances and scrap metal; and pays a licensed hazardous waste hauler to dispose of the PCBs.

State and local governments in conjunction with industry or a salvage company can establish recycling centers for refrigerants. An ordinance could require that any discarded refrigerator or air conditioner be brought to the recycling center for reclamation of CFCs. A deposit-refund system for new car air conditioners and refrigerators would help create the incentive to return these appliances as they are replaced. Utilities and companies that sell appliances often pick up old refrigerators. Local and state governments should ensure that CFCs, as well as PCB oils still found in old units, are removed before disposal or recycling of metal parts.

"If companies don't reclaim the CFCs in their equipment, they are doing to the atmosphere what Exxon did to the Arctic," the chief engineer at ThermaFlo, a small Springfield, Massachusetts company that specializes in refrigeration systems, told me. He is also inventor of a low cost, portable CFC reclamation and charging unit newly marketed by ThermaFlo. The unit removes and filters virtually all CFCs from any given refrigerant system. It can be used by service technicians repairing CFC air conditioners, refrigerators, and chillers to evacuate and store CFCs and then to recharge the units. Appliance companies like Sears and GE that pick up old appliances when delivering a new one can employ this kind of reclamation unit to recycle CFCs rather than venting them to the atmosphere. If they contract with private haulers to remove old refrigerators, Sears and GE corporate environmental policy should require the contractors to reclaim the CFCs.

Chlorofluorocarbons that were and are now being used will remain in Earth's atmosphere for another seventy-five to one hundred years, destroying the ozone layer. It is impossible to sift or filter them from the stratosphere. But it is not impossible to start making changes in the local and regional world around you.

- Vote conservation by supporting environmental legislation and legislators.
- Buy products without ozone-depleting chemicals wherever possible.
- Seek out auto repair shops that recycle CFCs.
- Recommend an appliance recycling ordinance to your local legislator.

At the moment, consumers don't have much choice with many products. We can't buy a refrigerator without CFCs or a computer that was not made with CFC solvents. But more products made with safe alternatives will be coming on the market over the next few years. As happened with aerosols in the 1970s, the CFC-free alternatives will probably be prominently advertised. Be prepared to pay more for the new substitutes and for some inconvenience, like traveling farther to find a service station with a CFC recycling unit for your car air conditioner.

None of these actions is difficult. They take awareness, some time, and considerable care. If substitute products cost more, is not the finite cost worth saving an infinitely precious gaseous membrane that enabled ancestral life to leave the sea and live on land?

RESOURCES

Guides to Action/Organizations

The League of Conservation Voters
2000 L Street NW, Suite 804
Washington, DC 20036
(202) 785-8683

Protecting Life on Earth: Steps to Save the Ozone Layer (1988)
Cynthia Pollack Shea
Worldwatch Institute
1776 Massachusetts Ave. NW
Washington, DC 20036
$4

Protecting the Ozone Layer: What You Can Do: A Citizen's Guide to Reducing the Use of Ozone-Depleting Chemicals (1988)
Environmental Defense Fund
257 Park Avenue South
New York, NY 10010
(212) 505-2100
$2

Saving the Ozone Layer: A Citizen Action Guide (1988)
Natural Resources Defense Council
40 West 20th St.
New York, NY 10011
(212) 949-0049
Free (includes Stratospheric Distress card)

Alternative Products and Services

Alliance for Responsible CFC Policy
1901 Fort Myer Drive
Arlington, VA 22209
(703) 841-9363

Appliance Recycling Centers of America
654 University Avenue
St. Paul, MI 55104
(612) 291-1100

EPA
Office of Air and Radiation
Washington, DC 20036
(202) 475-7496

Paper Goods
Pro-Environment Packaging Council
New York, NY
(212) 753-1690

ThermaFlo
3640 Main St.
Springfield, MA 01107
(800) 556-6015

Markets mobile CFC reclamation unit for refrigeration systems.

Industry Trade Associations

International Mobile Air Conditioner Association
3003 LBJ Freeway, Suite 219
Dallas, TX 75234
(214) 484-5750

Maintains list of air conditioning service shops that comply with its recommendations on safe repair of systems and use recycling equipment.

Mobile Air Conditioning Society
7425 Westchester Pike
Upper Darby, PA 19082
(215) 352-1345

Maintains list of air conditioning shops that recycle refrigerants from automotive air conditioners.

PART FIVE

Global Warming: The Greenhouse Effect

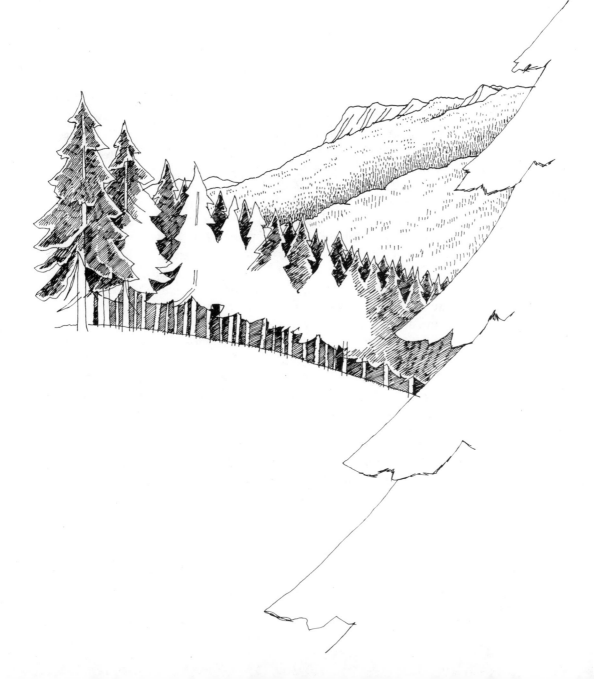

We have come to a threshold. If we cross this threshold, we may not be able to return.

Prime Minister Gro Harlem Brundtland of
Norway, Toronto Conference on the
Changing Atmosphere (1988)

*I*magine a translucent, vaporous blanket encircling and warming a planet enough to create an ambiance without peer in the solar system: one that supports life. For most of Earth's history a complex chemical exchange between atmosphere and ocean has achieved precisely this. A stratum of gases and clouds enables light to enter Earth's atmosphere and then absorbs and contains some of that solar energy as heat, much as glass does in a greenhouse. Without the "greenhouse effect" of this canopy of gases and clouds, the Earth would be about 40 to 60 degrees Fahrenheit colder than it is. Much of the planet would be frozen. The greenhouse effect is central to nature's strategy for equilibrating Earth's temperature, a function that is no less vital to life on our planet than the temperature of the human body is to our own life.

More than a hundred years ago, scientists theorized that carbon dioxide emissions from fossil fuel combustion would add to the greenhouse gases and increase their warming effect. During the past century atmospheric carbon dioxide has increased, most rapidly since the 1950s. That increase is consistent with a global warming trend over the same period.

Global temperature is higher today than it has ever been since 1862, the year climatologists first measured and recorded it with instruments. Record high temperatures have been reached *five times* during the 1980s: in 1980, 1981, 1983, 1987, and 1988. The rate of global warming for the past twenty years was greater than any in recorded history. A radical change in atmospheric temperature is ensuing. Climatologists who have simulated climate on other planets and past climates on Earth predict that hot summers, such as the summer of 1988, will occur more frequently during the 1990s in the United States: about 60 percent of the time, compared with 33 percent for the years 1950 through 1979. Droughts will comparably increase.

Many people associate global warming with discomfort, not changing climate. Predictions of a few degrees of average warming per century do not sound drastic. At worst, people think that the greenhouse effect will cause an energy crisis as more people turn up the air conditioner. Nor are we accustomed to thinking of heat and carbon dioxide as classic toxic pollutants like pesticides on our salad greens, lead in our drinking water, and hazardous waste buried in landfills or dumped into the sea.

But the trend of incremental global warming may be the most complex and potentially catastrophic of environmental issues we face. With some exceptions, scientists are reluctant to link specific drastic events, such as the summer heat wave and drought of 1988, to global warming. They speak in terms of "increased probability" and "frequency" of heat waves and drought. Almost all agree, however, that we cannot wait for absolute certainty that specific climate events are caused by global warming. Over the past fifteen years, climate researchers have predicted the natural phenomena that could result from the buildup of greenhouse gases:

- Drought in midcontinental areas (e.g., midwestern U.S.)
- More frequent and severe forest fires
- Flooding in India and Bangladesh
- Extended heat waves over large areas
- Superhurricanes

In 1988, the planet experienced all five.

MAAVELI

Chapter 14

The Causes and the Consequences

G ases are building up in the lower atmosphere primarily from industrial activities—gases such as carbon dioxide, the chlorofluorocarbons implicated in depletion of the ozone layer, ground-level ozone, nitrous oxide, and methane. They become part of the gaseous layer enshrouding the Earth, allowing solar radiation to enter Earth's atmosphere and trapping heat energy radiated back from the planet's surface. Emissions of carbon dioxide, or CO_2, account for approximately half of the warming trend—making CO_2 the largest single cause of the greenhouse effect.

Carbon dioxide is an essential component of the atmosphere and fundamental for life on Earth. The carbon dioxide content of the atmosphere has been kept constant over the life of our present atmosphere by a dynamic exchange between air and the oceans, which loosely hold huge reserves of carbon dioxide. Since the beginning of the Industrial Revolution in the late eighteenth century, the concentration of carbon dioxide in the atmosphere has increased by nearly 25 percent. Half of this increase has occurred since the 1950s, coinciding with worldwide industrial growth. Most of the excess carbon dioxide is formed and released in the combustion of coal, oil, natural gas, and gasoline.

Like the seas, forests—tropical, temperate, and boreal—are critical to nature's carbon dioxide economy. Trees take in carbon dioxide, chemically transform it, store the carbon, and then supply the air with oxygen. Rapid deforestation, in tropical rainforests in Central America, the Amazon River basin, Africa, and Southeast Asia, is removing nature's carbon dioxide storehouse or "sink" and thus is contributing to global warming. Enormous stands of trees are dying in Europe, Canada, and the United States from acid rain and air pollution. When removed, left to decay, or burned, trees release their stored carbon as carbon dioxide to the atmosphere. Recently a team of West German scientists found levels of air pollutants comparable to industrial areas over the virgin rainforests of Central Africa. Already under siege by development and lumbering, these forests are overhung year round with acid mists and ozone formed from annual humanmade brush fires. The fires, set to clear shrubs and stimulate crops and grass, rage for months across huge stretches of African savannas.

What of the other greenhouse gases? Chlorofluorocarbons or CFCs have up to 10,000 times the heat-holding capacity of carbon dioxide while they migrate through the lower atmosphere. They are a fraction of total greenhouse gases, yet they account for nearly 20 percent of global warming. Methane gas is generated by bacteria that decompose organic matter in oxygen-poor environments, and it is emitted most significantly from landfills, the digestive tracts of cattle, and fermenting rice paddies. Methane is also the principal component of natural gas. The concentration of methane gas in the atmosphere has doubled over the past two hundred years, an increase that is largely the result of the expansion of animal husbandry and rice cultivation, the enormous number of landfills, and leaking natural gas pipelines. Nitrous oxide is released to the atmosphere from nitrogen-based fertilizers and the combustion of fossil fuels and biomass. While ozone in the upper stratosphere is being depleted, ozone in the lower atmosphere is accumulating. Ground-level ozone is formed by the interaction of sunlight with pollutants such as nitrogen oxide discharged in auto exhaust.

The chemical composition of trace greenhouse gases in the atmosphere has changed in a small way, if we calculate only their concentrations. But in nature, minute changes produce mighty effects. These small changes, most scientists suspect, may alter climate drastically, induce great shifts in agricultural regions, add significantly to forest death, and raise sea levels substantially. Many agree with Gro Harlem Brundtland, chair of the World Commission on

Environment and Development, that we have come to a threshold across which there may be no return.

By the second half of the twenty-first century, average global temperatures may have increased as much as 3 to 10 degrees Fahrenheit at the current rate of buildup of greenhouse gases. The magnitude and rapidity of these temperature changes have never been experienced in human history. What are the possible results?

Global warming will cause the arctic ice sheets and alpine glaciers to warm and partially melt, the seas to expand, and sea levels to rise. By the year 2075, the seas will rise from 1 to 7 feet, depending on the magnitude of global warming. Many of the world's major cities are built on rich river deltas and coastal land with access to ports, harbors, and the sea. Even a sea level rise of 2 to 3 feet would have serious consequences for marine ecosystems, agriculture, and millions of people who reside near sea level. In the United States, rising sea levels could submerge most coastal wetlands, which are vital to the productivity of commercial fisheries. Shorelines and beaches would be eroded, coastal properties would be susceptible to storm damage, and drinking water sources would be contaminated by intruding salt water. Seven of the ten most populous U.S. cities are located either on coasts or coastal estuaries. By 1990, 75 percent of the country's population will reside on the coastal United States. For a 3-foot rise of sea level, estimates lie between $10 and $100 billion to maintain shorelines on the East Coast alone by measures such as diking cities.

A rise of 3 feet in sea level could flood 15 percent of the arable land in Egypt's Nile Delta. The same rise would flood 12 percent of low-lying Bangladesh and displace 11 million people. The tiny island of Maldives, home to 200,000, would be submerged and disappear. Approximately 50 percent of the world's population lives in coastal regions that would be threatened or inundated by rising seas. The numbers of environmental refugees would be staggering.

Local and regional climatic changes will be greater than global average ones. In the middle latitudes, where the continental United States is located, summer temperatures are expected to be 30 to 50 percent higher than the global average. It is likely that the interior of northern continents will become dryer and soils parched as temperatures rise and rainfall decreases. North America grain production currently provides a substantial portion of global grain reserves. Increased drought in the midwestern agriculture belt of the United States, as we experienced in summer 1988, could become commonplace: a catastrophe for world food supply and food prices.

Computer models suggest that, with global warming, monsoons may intensify in parts of southern Asia—all with profound consequence for rice growing and flooding, as suffered by Bangladesh in 1988. Many semiarid areas like sub-Saharan Africa, which have had severe droughts and famines for the last several decades, may experience even less rainfall.

In 1988, two congressional subcommittees held joint hearings on the Global Environmental Protection Act. Scientists working in many of the ecosystems that are affected by global warming described the consequences of incremental increases in global temperatures. Their testimony is sobering.

- Natural disasters such as "superhurricanes," could become increasingly common. An increase in sea surface temperatures from global warming could cause more intense hurricanes than we have ever seen in the past, with winds up to 225 miles per hour. Hurricanes develop from an interaction between the warmth and energy in the ocean's surface and the atmosphere. They arise when the water temperature at certain locations in the tropics rises above about 80 degrees Fahrenheit. Studies show that a temperature increase of a few degrees in tropical seas can lead to much more intense and frequent superhurricanes—ones like Hurricane Joan in 1988.

- Energy use caused by global warming could spiral upward. Higher temperatures will mean more fuel used to produce electricity for air conditioning. Using more fossil fuels will add more carbon dioxide, nitrogen oxides, and sulfur dioxide to the atmosphere. These pollutants will exacerbate ground-level ozone, acid rain, and global warming.

- Every one of 156 national forests is experiencing problems related to drought conditions, dry conditions being most critical in the West. Because of four consecutive years of drought in some parts of the country, with the year 1988 being the most widespread and severe, the moisture content of live and dead trees is at dangerously low levels—a condition that explains the insuppressible 1988 fire that burned 1.4 million acres of Yellowstone National Park. Drought makes it more arduous for young trees and grasses to repopulate burned regions and makes trees susceptible to attack by disease and insect. These biotic pressures come at a time when forests are suffering unprecedented death and decreased growth from acid rain and an atmospheric soup of air pollutants.

- Rapid global warming would affect mammals, especially large ones in the middle latitudes, causing reproductive failure. There would be wide-scale dwarfing and skeletal abnormalities and global mammalian extinction. Global warming would affect mammals as severely as did the last Ice Age, 11,000 years ago, when North America lost about 70 percent of its large animals.

- Global warming could set in motion a multitude of interactive feedback systems in nature. A second generation of effects may in turn slow or accelerate the initial change in climate. For example, as the Earth warms, forest growth will move toward the poles and replace ice, snow, and open tundra. Because of their greater potential to absorb radiation, forests in polar regions would further encourage the warming trend. On the other hand, more atmospheric carbon dioxide would cause plants to grow faster; in turn, they would take more carbon dioxide from the air and slow the warming trend. A warming trend, however, would also accelerate plant decay, which releases carbon dioxide and would thus accelerate global warming. Warmer ocean waters would absorb less carbon dioxide from ambient air and have less mixing with deep waters, thus removing and storing less atmospheric carbon dioxide. Warming would hasten the chemical tranformation of atmospheric methane to carbon dioxide, a more abundant but less damaging greenhouse gas, an effect that might slow global warming.

Warming seas, however, will increase the release of methane from marine sediments and intensify the warming trend.

The experts who testified before the congressional subcommittees concluded that, although we do not have in hand the precise connections between global warming and possible climate changes, **the major issue is not whether global warming will cause climate and ecological disasters, but how quickly they will occur.** Without a precise picture of the net effects of these physical and biochemical interactions in nature, many scientists agree that the multitude of small changes in nature caused by incremental global warming may have powerful effects. **We must take immediate action with what we know.**

The rise in greenhouse gases in the atmosphere is a direct consequence of modern development, principally from three activities: intensive fossil fuel combustion, the use of chlorofluorocarbons, and recent massive deforestation in the tropics. The current rate of greenhouse gas emissions will cause changes that may quickly outpace our ability to adapt to increased heat and drought, rising sea levels, and changes in agriculture. The emissions of greenhouse gases must be lowered in the near future to avoid catastrophic changes in climate, sea level, food production, and life on Earth. We must:

- Reduce net carbon dioxide emissions by: using energy more efficiently and developing renewable energy sources in place of fossil fuels.
- Phase out ozone-depleting and heat-absorbing CFCs.
- Stop massive destruction of forests, and plant trees in urban and rural areas of the temperate and tropical regions.

Nothing less than a concerted international effort to reorient energy use and industrial development is necessary. This environmental crisis—global warming with its attendant complex effects in nature—has demonstrated that global security is threatened by environmental pollution and degradation as much as by the prospect of "nuclear winter" after nuclear war. Every country must be involved in the effort to slow global warming because every country, by reason of agriculture and climate, will be affected by it.

But it is the industrialized countries that are most responsible for the problem. Before the recent massive burning of tropical forests, the forests of the north were destroyed. In the Middle Ages, the forests of western Europe were cleared. Much of the North American continent was rapidly deforested by European immigrants. Almost no great stands of primeval forest remain in the world's temperate zones, except in Canada and Siberia.

Industrial countries generate most of the greenhouse gases and also export the models of industrial development that are the sources of environmental degradation in developing countries. The average Indian, for example, uses only 4 percent of the energy consumed by the average citizen of the United States. In addition, U.S. consumers use energy more wastefully than the populations of other industrial nations. In 1985, 23 percent of total global carbon dioxide emissions originated in the United States, a country with only 5 percent of the world's population. The United States is the single largest carbon dioxide-emitting country and the highest per capita contributor to global warming in the industrial world. In 1986, the United States used 10 percent of its gross national product to pay the national fuel bill, whereas Japan used only 4 percent. For these reasons—that U.S. energy use is more intensive and less conserving per person than anywhere else in the world—the recommendations for change will focus here on what we in the United States can do to slow global warming. This emphasis upholds a principle championed by the Environmental Protection Agency and propounded in U.S. environmental law: **The polluter pays**.

RESOURCES

Reading/Information

The Global Environmental Protection Act of 1988: Joint Hearings Before the Subcommittee on Hazardous Wastes and Toxic Substances and the Subcommittee on Environmental Protection (September 14, 16, 1988)

U.S. Government Printing Office
732 North Capitol St. NW
Washington, DC 20402
(202) 275-3648

The Potential Effects of Global Climate Change on the United States (1988)
Report to Congress
U.S. Environmental Protection Agency
Washington, DC 20460
(202) 382-4700
$32

Chapter 15

Reducing Greenhouse Gases

The Union of Concerned Scientists advocates for a global policy to guard against the greenhouse effect. Like a good insurance policy, it should cost relatively little and carry other benefits as well, such as protecting the ozone layer and reducing air pollution.

Energy production based on carbon-rich fossil fuels is the principal cause of global warming. Fossil fuels are the relics of ancient plant and animal life that bound atmospheric carbon in their tissue. Thousands of years later, when we burn their decayed remains as coal, oil, gas, and gasoline, countless tons of carbon are released, principally as the greenhouse gas carbon dioxide. Fossil fuel combustion also releases chemicals and chemical precursors, oxides of nitrogen and sulfur, which cause ground-level air pollution: acid rain and ozone. With the Union of Concerned Scientists, I believe that the policy that best ensures against continued global warming ought to be an energy policy to reduce net CO_2 emissions in the least expensive methods possible.

Environmentalists and governments worldwide are of one mind on this objective. The 1988 Toronto Conference on the Changing Atmosphere recommended that the world reduce its CO_2 emissions more than 50 percent below present levels and set an initial goal of 20 percent by the year 2005. Sooner is better: Environmentalists recommend a reduction of 20 percent by 2000 and 30 percent by 2005. With that as our not-so-distant goal, what can we do to achieve it?

ENERGY CONSERVATION

Conserving energy—using less energy for the same activities—does not mean hardship. It means, first, getting higher efficiency from the energy we already use. Stretching the energy we consume by using it more efficiently can be the cornerstone of an energy policy that is effective, inexpensive, and protective of our environment. More than ten years ago, economists and energy experts in the Energy Project at the Harvard Business School concluded that conservation of energy was a largely untapped resource that could supply up to 40 percent of U.S. energy use at that time. The project's report was published in *Energy Futures*, widely read then because of a dramatic rise in world oil prices, the emergent geopolitics of oil, and the sudden realization that fossil fuel sources are finite. What oil reserves were left would be become more difficult and too expensive to extract, the authors argued.

Energy prices did not continue to grow at the exponential rate of the late 1970s; so some of the impetus to conserve was dampened in the 1980s. Between 1980 and 1988, the federal government cut the budget for renewable energy by 80 percent. In 1988, Transportation Secretary James Buckley rolled back the increase in federal fuel efficiency standards for 1989 automobiles and light trucks. Simultaneously, the Department of Energy proposed weak new refrigerator efficiency standards that would pass up an opportunity to conserve electricity and thus lower CO_2 emissions.

Even with these setbacks, energy conservation has already made more energy available *than any other single source*. Since the mid-1970s, energy conservation measures taken to avert an oil crisis have conserved a considerable amount of fossil fuels: the United States has had an increase of 35 percent in the gross national product without increasing energy consumption. If measures were taken to conserve on energy use in the United States so that we were as energy efficient as Japan, the United States would cut in half its energy use. For an investment of $50 billion per year, energy economists point out, a savings of $220 billion per year would be realized. The Natural Resources Defense Council puts the case for energy conservation through greater efficiency bluntly: "[North] America's largest unexploited oil and gas reserves lie not in environmentally sensitive coastal or Alaskan fields but in an enormous stock of inefficient automobiles, buildings and appliances."

Even more important is something not appreciated in the 1970s campaign to conserve oil: Cutting our energy use dramatically with already existing technologies in most cases will reduce carbon dioxide emissions and slow global warming. If they are taken, the actions discussed in this chapter and the subsequent chapters on reforestation will reduce CO_2 emissions at least 20 percent below 1987 levels by the year 2000 and 30 percent by 2005.

WHAT YOU CAN DO

---

1. Use Energy-Efficient Transportation.

Transportation accounts for about 30 percent of CO_2 emissions. The average fuel efficiency is 26.5 miles per gallon (mpg) for new U.S. cars and 19.5 mpg for new light trucks. At this rate, cars pump their own weight in carbon into the atmosphere each year. Some cars now on the market, however, get twice as many miles per gallon as that average, emitting half the CO_2. Some foreign manufacturers have developed even more economical cars that are getting over 100 mpg. Several innovative fuel-efficient automobiles achieve over 50 mpg; most are Japanese. In addition, the Volvo LCP 2000 is a four-passenger car that gets 63 mpg in the city and 81 mpg on the highway. Renault has recently tested a prototype vehicle that gets 124 mpg.

Environmentalists call for the government to raise the fuel economy standard for new cars from the current 26.5 to 48 mpg and for new trucks from 19.5 to 33 mpg by the year 2000. This action would save more than five times as much oil as the Interior Department says might be found in Alaska National Wildlife Refuge.

The Natural Resources Defense Council calculates that if new cars average 48 mpg and new trucks 33 mpg by the year 2000, U.S. CO_2 emissions could be reduced by 4 to 5 percent.

The Alza Corporation of Palo Alto, California pays its employees $1 for each day they bicycle to work. Twenty percent of the Xerox Corporation employees bike to work in Palo Alto. The company offers a towel service in the office shower room for bicyclists.

In their January 2, 1989 Planet of the Year issue, *Time* asked their readers if they would be willing to pay 50¢ per gallon more in gasoline in order to spur fuel conservation. By late June, 11,854 readers had responded: 9,136 for, 2,554 against, and 164 undecided.

The Economist argues that a realistic "pay-as-you-go" approach to using a natural resource would include the costs of rendering that resource more scarce and polluting other resources. "Translate that into hard cash, and what might you get? Water at $1 a gallon, perhaps, or petrol at $20 a gallon."

Public monies need to be aggressively invested in mass transit systems, including rail, bus, subway, and van pools, to reduce the number of miles people travel in private automobiles and to slow the growth in automobile ownership. Drivers almost never pay the full costs of their cars, which include road building and maintenance, noise, congestion, air pollution, and global warming. Some energy economists recommend that purchasers of efficient cars be rewarded with rebates, much as was done for alternative energy systems in the 1970s. Those who buy inefficient cars would pay a "gas guzzler" tax. Another proposal to fund mass transit and energy conservation programs is a "carbon fee" of at least $1 per gallon of gasoline. Even with an added carbon fee of one dollar per gallon, U.S. gasoline prices would still be lower than those of Japan and Europe.

If urban transit systems were optimized, annual U.S. CO_2 emissions could be reduced by 0.3 percent by the year 2000.

None of us has to wait for the government to raise efficiency standards in cars or to improve public transit in order to lower CO_2 emissions. "To reduce carbon dioxide worldwide, start right here," advises one regional transit authority administrator.

- Calculate how many miles you drove last year and drive 10 percent fewer miles this year by car pooling, using public transportation, and biking.

- Make your next car more fuel efficient than the current one. Choose one with a fuel efficiency of at least 30–35 mpg.

- Keep your car well tuned, so it is more fuel efficient and less polluting.

- Support legislation for a "carbon fee" on gasoline to encourage fuel conservation and fund mass transportation.

2. Make Your Home and Office Building Energy Efficient.

The building sector is the single largest consumer of energy—40 percent—in the economy. Seventy-five percent of the national elec-

Ask your local utility to do an energy audit of your home and business to recommend cost-effective ways to conserve energy.

tric demand comes from buildings. Most states could cut in half the energy needed to heat space and hot water by adopting standards in their building codes similar to those pioneered in California and the Pacific Northwest. Such codes regulate the amount of insulation in buildings and set standards of efficiency for central heating and cooling systems. They require that conservation measures that are cheaper than new energy supply be taken in building construction. The federal government could also adopt more rigorous building standards on insulation and heating and cooling systems for federal buildings and federally sponsored housing.

It costs no more to construct an energy-efficient office building than it does to construct an inefficient one. The savings on heating, cooling, and light would pay for insulation, smaller double-glazed windows, and automated controls for thermostats and lighting. If all new office buildings were built with these improvements in energy efficiency, we would have eliminated the need for eighty-five power plants and the equivalent of two Alaskan oil reserves—all with no investment.

What about homes? Since the mid-1970s fuel consumption in housing has dropped by about 30 percent. New "superinsulated" houses have achieved enormous energy savings, reducing fuel needs by more than 75 percent. They are built with heavily insulated walls and ceilings (R-30 and R-60, respectively), materials with thermal mass, double and triple-glazed windows and, often, ventilation systems that recover heat from exhaust air with air-to-air heat exchangers. Superinsulated houses hold and store the heat from people, lighting, appliances, and passive solar heating through south-facing windows.

State and local building standards for heating and cooling could reduce carbon dioxide emissions 2.3 percent by the year 2000.

3. Replace Inefficient Lighting.

Advances in electric light bulbs offer an important opportunity to use less electricity on lighting and thus lower carbon dioxide emissions from the generation of electricity. New bulbs and fluorescent lights use 75 percent less electricity than conventional

Seventh Generation catalogue advertises the 15-watt Marathon Light Capsule, which replaces a 60-watt incandescent bulb and will outlast nine standard incandescent bulbs.

ones by converting more of the electricity to light rather than heat.

As the government has encouraged conservation with insulation standards and efficiency standards in buildings and appliances, so it can strengthen lighting efficiency standards. The government should tighten model building codes to require the most efficient lighting and immediately strengthen efficiency standards for fluorescent ballasts, bulbs, and lamps. Utility companies can also provide incentives (see the example on Boston Edison) for the use of more efficient ballasts, replacement bulbs, and fixtures.

The adoption of tighter standards for commercial and residential lighting could reduce annual U.S. CO_2 emissions 1.3 to 2.5 percent by the year 2000.

❑ ❑ ❑

The Boston Edison *Efficient Lighting Program* offers rebates to commercial customers for going beyond building code or upgrading their existing lighting program. Commercial lighting can account for nearly 50 percent of an electric bill. This incentive program encourages replacement of old-fashioned lighting with new, energy-efficient lighting such as high-pressure sodium lamps, metal halide lamps, occupancy sensors, day lighting sensors, specular reflectors. With the rebate, customers often see a payback within a few months. Call your utility company to see if they have a rebate program for commercial customers.

❑ ❑ ❑

4. Buy Efficient Appliances.

One-third of the electricity produced in the United States is used in our homes for appliances, heating and cooling, and lighting. Refrigerators alone use the energy generated by twenty-five large power plants. The American Council for Energy-Efficient Economy calculates that if all households in the United States had the most efficient refrigerators on the market, twelve of the twenty-five large power plants would not be needed.

Appliances are already significantly more efficient than they were ten years ago. Federal regulations signed into law in 1987 mandate improvements in the efficiency of all major household appliances to be phased in over time. Stricter federal standards for feasible improvements, however, could triple the potential in energy savings.

The adoption of stricter standards for appliances could reduce annual U.S. CO_2 emissions by 2 to 3 percent by the year 2000.

You can help reduce CO_2 emissions by selecting the most energy-efficient appliances and buying with total energy costs and the environment in mind. Each household pays an average of $1,000 per year in energy costs for appliances such as refrigerators, freezers, stoves, dish and clothes washers, and heating and cooling equipment. High-efficiency appliances and space heating and cooling equipment will significantly lower energy bills. They may be slightly more expensive to buy, but the extra initial cost for a more efficient appliance is paid back through reduced energy bills long before the product wears out.

The least expensive appliance is not necessarily the cheapest one. The *lifecycle* of an appliance—that is, the combination of its purchase price and the annual operating costs over its lifetime—identifies the best buy (see Figure 15.1). Use this method of calculating lifecycle costs to purchase more efficient, more ecological, and ultimately less expensive appliances.

❏ ❏ ❏

In a study for Austin, Texas, Amory Lovins and colleagues from the Rocky Mountain Institute calculated that homes in Austin could save 63 percent of their electricity by employing a carefully chosen package of available technologies. These included compact fluorescent lights, double-glazed windows with film, efficient refrigerator and freezer, upgraded air conditioner, roof insulation, plugging air leaks, improved TV and minor appliances, efficient hot water tank. Energy savings would repay the costs of the retrofits within about three years (see the Resources section).

❏ ❏ ❏

United States industry is still much more energy intensive than the industries of Europe and Japan. The industrial use of energy can be improved in three ways.

Figure 15.1

COMPARISON SHOPPING AND LIFECYCLE COSTS

To compute a lifecycle cost, you will need to know:

1. The purchase cost (the price you pay from the appliance store).
2. The cost of energy (from your utility bill or your local utility).
3. The yearly energy cost to operate the appliance (obtained from the Energy Guide label).
4. The estimated lifetime of the appliance in years, given in Table 15.1.
5. A discount factor, a number that adjusts for inflation and for the fact that a dollar spent today does not have the same value as a dollar spent in the future, since today's dollar could be invested and earn interest over time. Discount factors are given in the table below.

The following formula is used to calculate lifecycle costs:

$$\text{Lifecycle cost} = \text{Purchase price} + \left\{ \text{annual energy cost} \times \text{estimated lifetime} \times \text{discount rate} \right\}$$

Table 15.1 Characteristics of Appliances for Lifecycle Cost Comparisons

Appliance	Average Lifetime (years)	Discount Factor*
Water heater (gas or electric)	13	0.83
Refrigerators and Freezers	20	0.76
Room air conditioners	15	0.81
Dishwashers	12	0.84
Clothes washers	18	0.78

*Based on a discount rate of 5% and increase in the price of energy of 2% per year above inflation.

Consider the following example: You want to do a lifecycle cost comparison between Refrigerator A and Refrigerator B. You call your local utility and learn that electricity costs 10 cents per kWh. You look at the Energy Guide labels on Refrigerators A and B. The Yearly Cost table toward the bottom of the Energy Guide label shows that at an electricity price of 10¢/kWh, Refrigerator A has an annual energy cost of $100 while Refrigerator B has an annual energy cost of $120. The price on model A is $600, and the price of model B is $520. You check the table on this page to find the correct lifetime (20 years) and discount factor (0.76) for refrigerators. With this information, you can now compare the lifecycle costs of the two refrigerators:

Appliances	Purchase price		Annual energy cost		Estimated lifetime		Discount factor		Lifecycle cost
Refrigerator A	$600	+	($100	×	20	×	0.76)	=	$2120
Refrigerator B	$520	+	($120	×	20	×	0.76)	=	$2344

From this calculation you learn that the refrigerator with the more expensive purchase price, model A, will actually cost you $224 less than the cheaper model over their lifetimes.

Use these worksheets to compare different models of appliances you are considering.

Worksheets for Computing Lifecycle Costs

Electricity price _____ ¢/kWh   Gas _____ ¢/therm
(Obtained from your utility bills or call your utilities)

Appliance Model	Purchase price	Annual energy cost	Estimated lifetime	Discount factor	Lifecycle cost
_____	_____ +(_____	× _____	× _____	) =	_____
_____	_____ +(_____	× _____	× _____	) =	_____
_____	_____ +(_____	× _____	× _____	) =	_____
_____	_____ +(_____	× _____	× _____	) =	_____
_____	_____ +(_____	× _____	× _____	) =	_____

Unfortunately, accurate lifecycle cost comparisons between different central air conditioners and furnaces must also include information concerning local climate and the condition of a home. Therefore, this procedure for computing lifecycle costs does not apply to these products.

SOURCE: *The Most Energy-Efficient Appliances*, 1988 ed. (Washington, DC: American Council for an Energy-Efficient Economy).

1. Installing equipment for capturing and using waste heat to do useful work.

2. Using equipment more efficiently: for example, turning off machines that are idle, or installing electronic speed controls on electromechanical drives.

3. Recycling materials like aluminum and reducing the intensity of materials, for example, building lighter cars.

Japan, which has substantially reduced energy use in industry, requires that companies above a certain threshold of energy use have a full-time energy manager. Does your company have one?

Innovative and dedicated promotion of industrial efficiency would reduce annual CO_2 emissions 2 to 4 percent by the year 2000.

5. Support Renewable Energy.

During the 1980s, financial incentives and research funds for renewable energy were cut by as much as 80 percent. Renewable energy has been treated as a "fringe" technology and dismissed as too expensive and not competitive with current energy sources. Were the full cost of using fossil fuels calculated, it would include the expensive problems they cause: global warming, oil spills, acid rain, air pollution, and damage to human health and ecosystems. Because these costs are hidden and not reflected in energy costs, and because government support for renewables has nearly vanished, renewable energy sources have not been given a fair chance to replace more polluting energy sources.

In 1985, renewable sources, including windpower, small-scale hydro, geothermal, biomass, and solar energy, accounted for almost 5 percent of total U.S. energy consumption. Since 1976, the price of photovoltaic cells, which convert sunlight directly to electricity, has dropped by a factor of 10. The world market for photovoltaics has grown fiftyfold. Experts predict that the price gap between utility-supplied electricity and photovoltaic cells will be bridged within a decade. Commercial uses of windpower and solar energy are proving their potential. In California, several 30-megawatt solar thermal electric plants supply electricity to utilities at competitive prices. The world market for wind turbines doubled every year from 1981 to 1985, reaching the equivalent of one coal-fired plant per year. All this has been developed without the government subsidies that nuclear power has enjoyed and the artificially low costs from which fossil fuels have benefited, because the tab for environmental damage they cause is picked up elsewhere.

If renewable sources were used to their capability, U.S. CO_2 emissions would be reduced 2.8 percent by the year 2000.

WHY NOT NUCLEAR POWER?

Nuclear power lost its future in the United States after the near meltdown of the Three Mile Island nuclear reactor in early 1979. The legacy of the atomic bomb, nuclear power was to have provided 30 to 40 percent of our electricity by the end of the 1980s and 50 percent by the twenty-first century. By 1980, U.S. utility officials virtually stopped ordering atomic-powered generating equipment. Dozens of nuclear power plant orders were canceled; twice as many were deferred. The paralyzing issues for the industry were economics (cost increases in nuclear construction have outpaced rises in construction costs in all other power industries); mounting public antipathy and activism; increased government regulation; and the changing prognostication of energy demand as efficiency and conservation measures were being taken. The issues for the public, after Three Mile Island particularly, were a fear of nuclear accident and nuclear waste; a disdain for the "acceptable risk" theory; and the association of nuclear power with nuclear weapons.

Global warming has revived government and industry hopes for nuclear power. Like renewable energy sources, it does not generate CO_2 nor contribute to global warming; so its advocates now portray it as almost ecological. I have heard supporters of nuclear power argue that radioactive waste disposal is no different a problem than naturally occurring radioactivity. Since we live with one, they ask, why can't we live with the other? But isn't this like saying that road salt in municipal drinking water is not a health issue because it is a natural substance, we even add it to food, and it doesn't cause cancer? The chronic problems of safety, cost, management, and disposal of radioactive wastes still plague nuclear power. Indeed, the problem of waste disposal has worsened. There are no ecological methods of destroying or disposing of nuclear waste. It is encapsulated and stored in perpetuity. How many communities in the United States will now accept a permanent nuclear storage facility within their boundaries? Fewer than in 1979.

Who will pay for the decommissioning of old reactors, and again, what will be done with the waste? Even if nuclear power plants become safer to operate in the future, that future may be too far off to affect global warming. Further, the waste still remains. Even those Western states that have accepted waste for permanent storage—New Mexico, Idaho, and Colorado—are shutting their doors. How will governments prevent the traffic in nuclear material from power plants to countries or terrorist groups that seek to develop nuclear weapons, when no waste—solid, hazardous, or nuclear—is fully secure from trade and trafficking?

Nuclear power plants coming on line today produce electricity at an average of twice the cost of new coal-fired plants. The full costs of nuclear power, including decommissioning and waste disposal, keep rising while the costs of renewable energy are decreasing. In a comparative analysis of nuclear power and energy conservation through energy efficiency, the Rocky Mountain Institute found that "electrical efficiency is nearly seven times more effective in abating CO_2 (per dollar invested in the United States) than nuclear power." Nuclear energy does not meet the criteria of a good global insurance plan against global warming.

In the 1970s, the oil embargo and the meteoric rise in oil prices created a crisis in fossil fuel-generated energy, a crisis that sparked public interest in energy conservation and renewable energy sources. This broad-based enthusiasm for saving finite nonrenewable fossil fuels coincided with a more idealistic alternative energy movement to "design with nature." A graduate student in engineering at the height of this movement, I was inspired to develop a prototype solar sunspace for my thesis topic. With the aid of a computer program, I designed a two-story passive solar greenhouse that could be retrofitted onto an existing building. To prove its potential, I built the solar sunspace onto my hundred-year-old rambling New England house. The next year, the house required—as predicted—25 percent less oil for heating. Two years later, I modified the design to build a new superinsulated passive solar house that uses only two cords of wood for heating and needs little cooling in summer. With minor changes, the house would require substantially less heating—as little as one-half to one cord of wood.

I love this house, particularly when the winter sun strikes deep into its south-facing rooms, warming them so thoroughly that no other energy source is needed. But today there is something deeper at issue than the considerable satisfaction of "designing with the sun." Our expansive use of fossil fuels is intimately connected with changes to the global atmosphere, air pollution and acid rain. It is killing forests, lakes, and fish, exacerbating lung illnesses, and now causing climate change. We must change these ways, not only to conserve finite reserves, but to reverse global warming and diminish air pollution. There is no time to wait.

Table 15.1 shows estimates developed by the Natural Resource Defense Council to reduce net 1987 U.S. CO_2 emissions by at least 20 percent by the year 2000 and 30 percent by the year 2005. The actions necessary are those discussed in this chapter and are referenced in the Resources section.

Reforesting our Earth is a critical component of saving our atmosphere: Some scientists estimate that a full third of global warming is the result of deforestation. For peoples of the forests who have lived for centuries from the forests without destroying them, deforestation means the entire loss of their economy and their way of life. The next two chapters show how we can reforest the Earth.

Table 15.1 Actions to Reduce Net 1987 U.S. CO_2 Emissions by at Least 20% (figures shown represent midpoints of ranges based on initial NRDC estimates)

Action	Reduction in U.S. CO_2 Emissions By Year 2000	Reduction in U.S. CO_2 Emissions By Year 2005
	(percent)	*(percent)*
Energy		
Federal vehicle fuel efficiency standards	4.4	5.6
Federal commercial lighting efficiency standards	2.1	3.9
Federal actions to improve residential lighting	0.4	0.4
Federal appliance efficiency standards	2.5	3.5
Federal actions to promote industrial efficiency	2.8	5.3
State and local building efficiency standards	2.3	3.5
Improvements in mass transit	0.3	0.6
Actions to promote renewable energy sources	2.8	4.0
Subtotal	17.6	26.8
Forestry		
Federal conservation reserve forestry program	1.4	1.4
Actions to increase timber growth on nonindustrial private forest lands	1.5	1.5
Improved management of national forests	0.4	0.4
Urban tree planting	1.2	1.2
Subtotal	4.5	4.5
TOTAL	22.1	31.3

SOURCE: *Cooling the Greenhouse: Vital First Steps to Combat Global Warming* (New York: Natural Resources Defense Council, 1989).

RESOURCES

Guides to Action/Organizations

Advanced Electricity-Saving Technologies and the South Texas Project (1987)
Rocky Mountain Institute
1739 Snowmass Creek Rd.
Snowmass, CO 81654
(303) 927-3128
$95

Building on Success: The Age of Energy Efficiency (1988)
Christopher Flavin and Alan B. Durning
Worldwatch Paper 82
Worldwatch Institute
1776 Massachusetts Ave. NW
Washington, DC 20036
$4

Cooling the Greenhouse: Vital First Steps to Combat Global Warming (1989)
Recommendations for U.S. Policies and Actions
Natural Resources Defense Council
1350 New York Avenue NW, Suite 300
Washington, D.C. 20005
(202) 783-7800
$5

"How You Can Fight Global Warming"
Union of Concerned Scientists
26 Church St.
Cambridge, MA 02238
(617) 547-5552

UCS produces both printed and video educational materials on a variety of energy and defense-related issues, including the greenhouse crisis.

Slowing Global Warming: A Worldwide Strategy (1989)
Christopher Flavin
Worldwatch Paper 91
Worldwatch Institute
1776 Massachusetts Ave. NW
Washington, DC 20036
$4

Alternative Products

The Most Energy-Efficient Appliances
American Council for an Energy-Efficient Economy

1001 Connecticut Ave. NW, Suite 535
Washington, DC 20036
(202) 429-8873
$2

This annual booklet lists the most energy-efficient residential appliances, including refrigerators, freezers, clothes washers, dishwashers, furnaces, boilers, water heaters, air conditioners, heat pumps available in the United States. ACEEE also publishes *Saving Energy and Money with Home Appliances*, a 34-page guide to the purchase and use of energy-efficient appliances. $2

Resource-Efficient Housing Guide (1989)
Rocky Mountain Institute
1739 Snowmass Creek Rd.
Snowmass, CO 81654
(303) 927-3851
$15

A select annotated bibliography and directory of helpful organizations.

Seventh Generation catalogue
10 Farrell St.
South Burlington, VT 05403
(802) 862-2999
$2

Water-conserving toilet dam and shower heads; energy-efficient lighting, solar-powered devices, etc.

Reading/Information

"Costing the Earth: A Survey of the Environment" (1989)
The Economist
$4

To order, call Bradley Cleaton, (212) 541-5730.

"Global Warming: Policy Options" (July 1988)
Susan Hassol
IRT Supplement, A Strategic Newsbrief for the Electric Utility Industry
IRT Publications
P.O. Box 10990
Aspen, CO   81612-9689
(303) 927-3155
$295 annually for profit-making companies; $195 for nonprofits

No Immediate Danger: Prognosis for a Radioactive World (1985)
Dr. Rosalie Bertell
The Women's Press
124 Shoreditch High St.
London EI 6J3, England
£5.95

Chapter 16

Agriculture in a Warmer World

For all its technological progress, [North] American agriculture still remains at the mercy of the weather.
Natural Resources Defense Council, *Farming in the Greenhouse* (1989)

The futility of farming in the bleak, bone-dry Dust Bowl of the Depression era is immortalized in Margaret Bourke-White's photographs of migrant farm families and John Steinbeck's *The Grapes of Wrath*. Recent droughts are coinciding with years of record-high global temperatures to produce summers like that of 1988, when unrelenting hot, dry weather gripped nearly half of the United States. Farming survived, but not without substantial losses in grain harvests and forage grasses for farm animals. Farming survived, in part thanks to a multibillion dollar relief package—the largest disaster relief measure in U.S. history.

Half of land in the United States produces crops and nourishes livestock. One in five people in the private workforce work in some part of the agriculture sector: growing, distributing, and processing food products. Called the "bread basket" of the world, U.S. farmland produces enough wheat and coarse grain to supply half the world's total grain exports. More frequent summer drought and heat bodes ill for world food supply, especially for people of developing countries, who have been made more and more dependent on food imports.

Climatologists have only an imprecise understanding of what changes in climate we will experience with rising world temperatures. Although they expect an increase in average precipitation throughout the globe, they also predict more frequent droughts and heat waves in the United States. The National Aeronautics and Space Administration's analysis suggests that the number of hot summers in the 1990s will double compared with the period 1950 through 1979. Droughts will increase similarly. What are the implications for agriculture?

Heat and water stress during the critical days of flowering can devastate corn. Higher than usual temperatures prevent wheat from maturing properly. The food supply for farm animals—hay from pastures and rangeland, and corn—will be rapidly depleted by more repeated hot, dry summers. Figure 16.1 portrays the recent rapid and frequent decline in U.S. corn yields. The 1988 drought—showing the most precipitous drop in corn production—reduced corn, wheat, and soybean yields from 1987 levels by 34 percent, 14 percent and 21 percent, respectively. In July 1989, the governor of North Dakota appealed for federal emergency funds for farmers, saying the drought of 1988 never ended in that state. No one can prove incontrovertibly that the droughts of the 1980s are a consequence of global warming. But why wait for that proof, if waiting might take us over the threshold to erratic and drastic climate change?

Even without increasing drought, global warming will still exacerbate droughtlike conditions. Warmer temperatures will increase rates of soil moisture evaporation and plant transpiration. Surface water levels will drop from increased evaporation. The Texas State Department of Agriculture has estimated that an average increase of 7 degrees Fahrenheit would cause so much loss of water through evaporation-transpiration that very little precipitation would remain to recharge rivers, streams, lakes, and aquifers. With warmer winter temperatures, there may be less snow and more rapid spring snowmelt. These effects would result in less recharge to soil and groundwater and greater surface water runoff to rivers and streams.

Higher temperatures and more protracted summers may weaken the ability of crops to withstand insect attack and may aggravate plant damage from air pollution. Many plant pests tend to grow faster with increased temperature. Insect infestations may be another severe consequence of global warming for agriculture. The 1988 soybean crop, for example, was infested with spider mites that caused an estimated crop loss of 15 to 20 percent. The local air pollutant ozone kills plant leaves and reduces crop growth. Many experiments suggest that an increase of ozone pollution with high

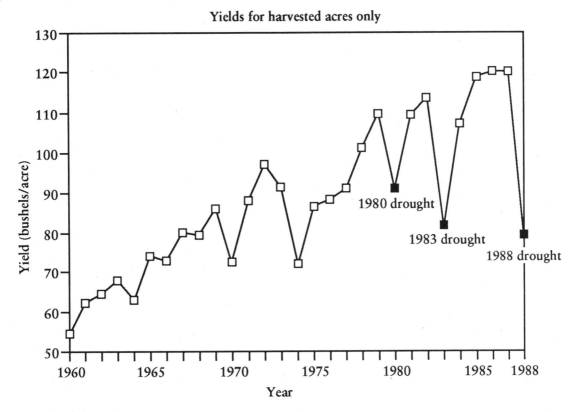

Figure 16.1 U.S. Corn Yield

SOURCE: *Farming in the Greenhouse: What Global Warming Means for American Agriculture*
(New York: Natural Resources Defense Council, 1989).

temperatures will cause increased losses in agricultural crops. The
World Resources Institute predicts that a doubling of lower atmosphere ozone could cut in half yields of ozone-sensitive plants, such
as peanuts and soybeans.

One school of thought, however, takes a different view. Simply
put, their theory states that the trend in global warming from a carbon dioxide-enriched atmosphere will enhance agriculture. Researchers have demonstrated in laboratories that plants grow faster
with increased carbon dioxide and that some crops use water more
efficiently. Added warmth can increase the rate of photosynthesis.

Thus, more warmth and more carbon dioxide will increase agricultural yields.

But the complexities of ecosystems suggest a less linear response from nature. In dry conditions, plants constrict their pores to reduce water loss, an effect that also tends to reduce their intake of carbon dioxide. Although plant growth increases with increased carbon dioxide, this growth spurt may be canceled out with higher temperatures, which cause plants to respire more and to assimilate less carbon dioxide above a critical temperature. If certain agricultural crops thrive in a carbon dioxide-enriched atmosphere, so will certain weeds as well. U.S. agriculture, already heavily herbicide dependent, will only become more so, thereby magnifying risks to health and ecosystems, if plants thrive with global warming. On a more speculative plane, plants in this new atmosphere may be more carbon enriched, less nutritious, and more attractive to herbivorous insects.

Can we afford to risk agriculture with a "wait-and-see" attitude toward the impact of global warming? The U.S. Department of Agriculture apparently thinks so. Using the euphemism "CO_2 fertilization," USDA does not see any serious risks to national agriculture from a warming trend. Their optimism rests on three assumptions: (1) Agriculture can shift to more northern states; (2) irrigation can compensate for dryer soil conditions; and (3) plant breeding can provide plant versatility for changing conditions. These turnkey solutions gloss over the rigors of any and all of these three adaptations.

What happens to the farms, farmers, and farming infrastructure left behind in the shift north of the "bread basket"? The soils of the northern Great Lakes region are not the rich loam of the agricultural heartland. Having inferior water-holding capacity and low amounts of organic matter, they are not ideal for agriculture. Finite water supplies, especially in the arid West, already have created tremendous political disputes over water rights. An agriculture increasingly dependent on irrigation because of heat and drought will only aggravate regional water shortages. Last, many scientists and environmentalists question the realism of expecting plant breeding to compensate for a spate of problems that are yet unpredictable.

Because of feedback mechanisms, climate changes may happen with a rapidity that leaves agronomic advances trailing.

WHAT CAN BE DONE?

Agriculture is only one of many planetary systems that are endangered by global warming. In itself, this vital sector warrants immediate action. The Environmental Defense Fund and the Natural Resources Defense Council recommend three crucial initiatives that should be taken to help protect U.S. agriculture from dislocation that could come with a warming trend. They are: (1) reforestation on marginal croplands; (2) soil and water conservation; and (3) plant research and planning. The recommendations are discussed in some detail in the studies listed in the Resources section. We explore here the potential for reforestation on marginal croplands because it forms part of an integral solution to global warming: *reforesting the Earth.*

Forests on Marginal Croplands

Forests are central to the carbon cycle and necessary for the thermal equilibrium of Earth. They take in carbon dioxide, the major greenhouse gas, and convert carbon into leaves and roots and store it in wood for centuries. The forest canopy allows carbon-rich organic material to accumulate and decompose, enriching soil. The rate at which forests absorb carbon dioxide varies with the mix of species, their growth and respiration rates, and cultivation practices. In general, 1 acre of growing forest can absorb about 8 tons of carbon dioxide per year, roughly the amount released in burning 3 tons of coal or 1,000 gallons of gasoline. Once established, within one or two decades 10 million acres of forest—an area roughly half the size of Indiana—would absorb some 80 million tons of CO_2 emissions, or 1.4 percent of total United States CO_2 emissions.

The Natural Resources Defense Council advocates that 10 million acres of forest be established on marginal cropland throughout the country as part of a concerted program to stem global warming and also to benefit eroding agricultural soil. This forestation could take place within an already existing federal program to preserve and restore eroding agricultural fields—the Conservation Reserve Program—administered by the U.S. Department of Agriculture. The CRP program aims to restore millions of acres of eroding agricultural fields by establishing tree, shrub, or native grass cover. Farmers who participate in the program receive ten years of "rental" payments as well as financial assistance to establish the cover vegetation.

Besides removing significant quantities of atmospheric carbon dioxide, forests on marginal croplands hold soil from eroding and they enhance the water storage capacity of soils. They are a biotic ecosystem attracting wildlife and providing a cooler microclimate. A source of wood, forests established on marginal croplands may relieve logging pressures on national forests.

This program's potential to restore forests on marginal agricultural land is elaborated on in both the EDF and the NRDC reports. Both point up the particular incentives that must be built into the Conservation Reserve Program to encourage and enable farmers to plant mixed species of trees rather than grasslands or monocultures of one tree variety. They advise that newly established forests contain tree species at the northern edges of their ranges to enable trees to adjust to climate changes: white oak in Minnesota, for example, bald cypress in southern Illinois, longleaf pine in North Carolina, and black mangrove in Florida.

Most of us do not farm—and can only support the Conservation Reserve Program. But as Chapter 17 demonstrates, many of us can influence, through direct and indirect means, the trend in deforestation worldwide. We can avoid buying the exotic woods taken from rainforests. We can boycott beef from cattle grazing on former rainforest. We can treat trees as if they are more than "wood."

RESOURCES

Reading/Information

Farming in the Greenhouse: What Global Warming Means for American Agriculture (March 1989)
Justin R. Ward, Richard A. Hardt, and Thomas E. Kuhule
Natural Resources Defense Council
1350 New York Avenue NW, Suite 300
Washington, DC 20005
(202) 783-7800
$5.50

Offsetting New CO_2 Emissions (September 1988)
D. Dudek
Environmental Defense Fund
257 Park Avenue South
New York, NY 10010
(212) 505-2100
$10

Chapter 17

Reforest the Earth

"Trees are not wood," Dr. Vandana Shiva, an Indian scientist, told the Congress on the Fate and Hope of the Earth in Nicaragua as she described the Chipko movement in her country to save trees. Trees are part of a diverse living world of plants and animals that offer medicine, food, fuel, and shelter to those who live near and in them. They are home to more species of plants, insects, and animals than any other ecosystem. Indian women who understand this have embraced trees so loggers could not cut them; they have placed themselves between chain saws and trees where intense logging was destroying primeval forests; they have formed human chains across logging roads to keep out logging equipment.

What kind of person hugs a tree? Someone who knows that nature is a day-to-day source of every aspect of her own and her community's life. She may not know the specific biochemical connection between trees and global warming—that trees absorb the principal "greenhouse gas," carbon dioxide. But she does know that trees temper climate and refresh air; that forests near her village are an ongoing supply of food, herbal remedies, and firewood. She has witnessed soil erosion and increased floods where hills have been shorn of trees. For these reasons, women and children stopped seventy lumberjacks from felling trees by wrapping their arms around the trees. This event, in 1974, began the Chipko movement.

Before the rainforests began to be slashed and burned so extensively in Amazonia, Southeast Asia, West Africa and Central America, European settlers cut and cleared enormous swaths of U.S. temperate forest. The eastern United States up to the Mississippi River and even beyond was once covered with dense forest. Only in the Pacific Northwest, including the temperate rainforests of the Olympic Peninsula in Washington and Alaska, do ancient or "old-growth" trees, as they are called, still exist. Even they may be gone in a few decades as the Forest Service permits timber companies to cut these trees. Saplings planted today can hardly replace three-hundred-year old trees.

The Wilderness Society estimates that up to 3.1 million Forest Service acres need to be reforested. In the southeastern United States, the American Forestry Association, a conservation group whose members include foresters and woodland owners, has identified 20 million open acres that could be planted to forest again. In a national campaign to reverse the greenhouse effect, the AFA has called for planting 100 million trees in yards and parks, around businesses and city buildings, and along streets by 1992. Numbers aside, we can simply think of a new tree planted for every two people in the United States—not monocultures but diverse woodlands and forests, where possible.

Deforestation brings soil erosion, floods, clogged and turbid streams, and extremes of climate, whether in the eighteenth-, nineteenth-, or twentieth-century United States or in the equatorial band of tropical rainforests. When forests are destroyed, habitats vanish; animals leave or become extinct. Deforestation is a critical factor in global warming, for the carbon dioxide that would have been absorbed and stored by trees is left to accumulate in the gaseous thermal blanket of the lower atmosphere. Trees cut and left to decay release their carbon as carbon dioxide.

Reforesting the Earth Begins at Home.

- Wanagri Maathai founded the Green Belt Movement in Kenya, a broad-based community tree-planting campaign, when she planted seven symbolic trees in 1977. The biologist observed the desert spreading when trees removed for fuel were not replaced. Then springs dried up without trees and soil water levels dropped. Using the tree as a focal point of environmental protection, she catalyzed a movement that has involved school children and 15,000 small-scale farmers, many of them women, who have planted more than 2 million trees. The trees are planted as a community woodland that Maathai calls a "green belt"; each green belt must have at least 1,000 trees. The tree-planting projects have stimulated rural employment and community environmental education.

- The American Forestry Association, a citizen conservation organization, has undertaken a national campaign, called Global Releaf, aimed at planting 100 million trees in cities and towns by 1992. Amway, the 1989 recipient of the Environmental Achievement Award of the United Nations Environmental Program, is the first company to join Global Releaf. Amway has supplied 13,000 seedlings to employees and top distributors and is encouraging its 1 million distributors in forty countries and territories to plant trees.

- The Massachusetts Re-Leaf program was announced on Arbor Day, 1989. Over the next decade 15,000 medium-sized trees will be planted in urban areas and 150,000 seedlings in state forests. The costs of the program will be paid by Massachusetts businesses as compensation for damage to the environment caused by their development projects or their violation of antipollution laws.

- Applied Energy Services of Arlington, Virginia is contributing $2 million toward the planting of 52 million trees over 385 square miles in Guatemala. The number of trees planted will be able to absorb the estimated 15 million tons of carbon dioxide emitted over the lifetime of a new 180 megawatt–generating plant the company is building in Uncasville, Connecticut. The full costs of tree planting are shared by the industry, international and national agencies, and the government of Guatemala. Some 40,000 small farmers in Guatemala will be involved in planting the trees on plantations and on small plots.

- On July 20, 1989, the prime minister of Australia pledged that 1 billion trees will be planted throughout Australia before the year 2000.

WHAT YOU CAN DO

1. Write the American Forestry Association about participating in Global Releaf (see Resources).

2. Talk to the Conservation Commission, the tree officer and the Department of Parks in your city or town, and the biology teacher of your community school about starting a tree-planting campaign.

3. Ask your employer to sponsor a tree-planting campaign by purchasing seedlings to be planted by children in a local school.

4. Remember: Planting trees is easy. Caring for saplings is critical.

5. Recycle paper: The average American consumes the equivalent of five trees annually.

In 1987, an environmental group called the Rainforest Action Network ran an ad campaign against Burger King and asked people to boycott the fast-food chain until the company stopped using imported beef from Costa Rica. The campaign slogan read: "Is it worth losing half the world's rainforests for 5¢ off a burger?" What is the circuitous connection between cheap fast food and rainforests?

Rainforests comprise less than 7 percent of the planet surface, and most lie within the tropical regions of Central and South America, West Africa, and Southeast Asia. These oldest ecosystems on

Earth are also the most productive, complex, and rich. Within them live almost half of all animal, plant, and insect species and more than a thousand tribes of forest people. The rainforest is the Earth's pharmacy: Seventy percent of 3,000 plants identified by the National Cancer Institute as having anticancer properties are rainforest species. Medicines to treat glaucoma, Hodgkin's disease, amoebic dysentery, lymphocytic leukemia, heart ailments, and hypertension are derived from plants that inhabit the rainforest. Even so, only 1 percent of rainforest plants have been studied by Western medicine, although forest peoples have wide knowledge of their healing properties.

In the past three hundred years, but mostly in the past forty years, half of the world's rainforests have been destroyed. The burning and cutting goes on at an intense rate, estimated at 35 to 100 acres per minute and 23,000 square miles per year. At this pace, all tropical rainforests will disappear within seventy-five years. Amazonia, the watershed of the immense Amazon River and its tributaries, is home to fully half of the 60 million species of life on Earth. By August 1988, nearly 12 percent of the Amazon rainforest had been torched and destroyed for farms, cattle ranches, dams, roads, and mining.

Why would the Rainforest Action Network stage hundreds of protests at Burger King franchises and even run a full-page ad in the *New York Times* asking readers to pressure the company to stop destroying rainforests of Central America? Much of Latin American forest has been destroyed over the past twenty-five years to market exotic woods and to create land for cattle grazing. Beef from Central American cattle that graze on once-fertile rainforest is sold to the United States for luncheon meats, baby foods, pet foods, and hamburgers. Fast-food chains save 5¢ wholesale on a hamburger using less expensive imported beef instead of domestic beef.

For every fast-food hamburger from Central American cattle, about 55 square feet of rainforest is destroyed. What life might this 55 square feet sustain, ask biologist Christopher Uhl and ecologist Geoffrey Parker. This patch of forest—the size of a small room—might contain a 60-foot tree, below which are some fifty saplings and seedlings in some twenty to thirty different species, some rare and found only in this habitat. Thousands of insects of a hundred species, some yet unknown, inhabit the vegetation. Dozens of bird, reptile, and mammal species would visit and browse in this 55 feet of forest. An uncountable mass of mosses, fungi, and microorganisms would live on leaf surfaces, bark, roots, and the soil. Altogether, conclude Uhl and Parker, millions of individuals and thousands of species inhabit the small space of rainforest destroyed to make a hamburger.

Nor is it likely that the pasture will sustain the cattle or the forest will regenerate when the pasture is abandoned. Rainforest is slashed and burned to create pasture for cattle. Within six to eight years, the grazed land is depleted of nutrients and unproductive as pasture. It is abandoned; more abundant, "cheap" forest is cleared. Once abandoned, these lands return to forest only slowly and may never contain their original species.

A world rainforest movement has arisen comprising people from the Northern and Southern Hemispheres who share a common urgency to rescue the temperate and tropical forests remaining from the enormous pressures to destroy them. For some—peoples of the forest—the endangered forest is their home, their sustainable livelihood, and their spiritual basis. For those living nearby, forests conserve soils, help regulate the hydrological cycle, and provide a source of fuel. For all of us, however remote from them, forests regulate climate at both the regional and global level. Ultimately, the rainforests are home to most other species of the Earth. The loss of the world's forests to economic development schemes like ranching, dams, mining, and industry, to industrial forestry, or to tourism constitutes a global tragedy and a global emergency—so much so that people place themselves between chain saws and trees.

Large intergovernmental issues are at stake here. For one, funding for Third World development programs from international aid agencies and banks has subsidized projects—dams, cattle ranching, mining, and logging operations—that destroy rainforest. A second issue is how to initiate models of sustainable development in all countries—the industrial ones as well as those containing the world's rainforests—whereby *economic decisions serve social and ecological ends*. Harvesting forests, for example, by nut collecting or rubber tapping, creates many more jobs than logging and also sustains the rainforest. Yet another issue is something called the "debt-for-nature swap," in which a third party, such as the Nature Conservancy, buys a portion of a developing country's debt and re-invests the debt in the natural resources of that country. This enables a debtor nation to invest in conservation of rainforests instead of depleting its resources for quick cash to pay off its debt.

Concurrent with the international issues are a multitude of local initiatives with global repercussions. The movement to save the rainforests is generating creative campaigns organized by groups worldwide. As individuals, we can take part in campaigns and exert personal action that is both political and powerful. After the successful campaign to force Burger King to stop buying beef raised on rainforest, the Rainforest Action Network began an international campaign with other advocates for tropical rainforests and indigenous peoples against Scott Paper Company. Scott Paper was planning to convert up to 2 million acres of Indonesian tropical rainforest and savanna, encompassing the homelands of 15,000 indigenous people, into tree plantations and a pulp project to make toilet paper and facial tissue. The groups urged Scott to devote its considerable resources to recycling and to get out of the business of destroying rainforest. In fall 1989, Scott Paper announced its withdrawal from the project.

What fast-food hamburgers are to the Central American rainforests, disposable chopsticks are to the rainforests of Southeast Asia. In Malaysia, chopsticks were traditionally handed down from grandmother to mother to child. A pair of chopsticks lasted one hundred years. Today the Malaysian rainforests are being clearcut by Japanese lumber companies to make 20 million pairs of throwaway chopsticks per year.

Herein lies an opportunity to think globally and act locally.

WHAT YOU CAN DO

The Body Shop, a company that sells skin lotions and oils that are not tested on animals, has numerous sustainable projects in the Third World. The founding owner, Anita Roddick, is working with an ethnobiologist to purchase herbs from rainforests for use in her products.

Ben and Jerry's has started a new company that will make nut brittle from nuts harvested from the rainforests in Brazil. The company plans to buy 150,000 pounds of nuts annually for their product, Rainforest Crunch. Forty percent of their profit will be donated to organizations that protect rainforests.

1. Write the rainforest organizations listed in the Resources section to join their latest campaigns to save forests and the traditional land rights of tribal peoples.

2. Support passage of a "beef labeling" act so that beef from rainforest-fed cattle must be marked accordingly.

3. Curb the wastage, misuse, and overconsumption of wood products.

4. Do not buy imports of tropical timber from natural forests, such as teak and rosewood, or tropical wood products.

5. Buy only those rainforest products, such as fruits, nuts, oils, flours, and rubber, that are produced from the living rainforest.

RESOURCES

Guides to Action/Organizations

Global Releaf
American Forestry Association
P.O. Box 2000
Department GR2
Washington, DC 20013

Rainforest Action Network
301 Broadway
San Francisco, CA 94133
(415) 398-4404

Reforest the Earth Project
48 Bethel St.
Norwich
Norfolk NR2 1NR, United Kingdom

World Rainforest Movement
87, Cantonment Road
10250 Penang, Malaysia

Reading/Information

Our Common Future (1987)
The World Commission on Environment and Development
Gro Harlem Brundtland, Chair
Oxford University Press
$9.95

State of the World
Annual Report on the Global Environment
Lester Brown et al.
Worldwatch Institute
1776 Massachusetts Ave.
Washington, DC 20036
(202) 452-1999
$9.95/copy; discount on larger orders

Afterword

It was a spring afternoon in West Florida. Janie had spent most of the day under a blossoming pear tree in the backyard. She had been spending every minute she could steal from her chores under that tree for the last three days. That was to say, ever since the first tiny bloom had opened. It had called her to come and gaze on a mystery. From barren brown stems to glistening leaf-buds; from the leaf-buds to the snowy virginity of bloom. It stirred her tremendously. . . . It was like a flute song forgotten in another existence and remembered again. . . . This singing she heard had nothing to do with her ears. The rose of the world was breathing out smell.

Zora Neale Hurston, *Their Eyes Were Watching God* (1937)

On Earth Day, 1970, 20 million people took to the streets in what was the largest political demonstration in U.S. history. They walked into polluted rivers with scuba gear, demonstrated at stockholders' meetings of corporate polluters, and conducted peaceful actions in front of the Department of Interior. Ten thousand schools, 2,000 colleges and universities, and almost every community took part. The U.S. Congress formally adjourned so that senators and representatives could attend teach-ins in their districts. That afternoon I took my twenty-five eleven-year-old students to walk along the Brandywine Creek, which bifurcates Wilmington, Delaware. Maybe we picked up trash, maybe we just walked on the cobbly streambank—I don't remember.

The kids were mostly from the older, struggling east side of Wilmington and the younger, uglier, angrier projects off Northeast Boulevard. They were second-class people in a state that purported to have the highest per capita income and the highest number of PhDs per capita in the United States. Downtown Wilmington, a stone's throw from where we walked, was embellished with the Hotel Du Pont and the Du Pont Office Building. Otherwise, it was a city of *de facto* segregated housing and segregated schools. A few years earlier, the National Guard had policed the streets, so raw and so threatening was the anger of urban Afro-Americans.

I remember asking myself, as I watched kids jumping from stream boulder to stream boulder: *What does this have to do with them?* What do clean streams have to do with literacy, jobs, housing, and human dignity?

Soon after, we held a schoolwide talent show. A lot of my students formed groups to do Motown songs with improvised steps. One boy asked to be in the show but didn't want to disclose his act. I inserted him between Motown skits, deeply curious (and a little anxious) about what this reticent, bookish child would do. When his turn came, James stood with his hands in his pockets and whistled bird songs. I have heard lovelier songs since, from birds themselves, but never before. Now I wait for the wood thrush to return each May and infuse the summer woods with its liquid flute songs, long after the red-winged blackbird, the robin and eastern bluebird, the catbird and phoebe have returned—because I have learned to listen for them. I can close my eyes and remember—not the songs—but the soft, startled feeling the boy's songs gave me. Rachel Carson called this rapid, light lifting above ordinariness to a place of the spirit "where the rose of the world was breathing out smell"—the *sense of wonder.* Everyone must have felt this same wondrous uplifting, because James won the talent show.

This child answered in part my pondering on the Brandywine— *what does Earth Day have to do with them?* Time, events, and a more complex understanding have helped to finish finding the answer.

- Earth Day is about rich nations sitting down with poor nations to forgive debt, because the rich nations have borrowed from the Earth's commonly held ecological systems, such as clean air, and left in its place the "junk" of acid rain and greenhouse gases. Earth Day is about the environmental debt that industrial nations have incurred in order to finance their economic development and wealth.

- Earth Day is about the urban poor, because environmentalism is not fundamentally the privileged cause of the upper class. It is the necessary issue of the poor. A recent church study found that blacks and Hispanics are more likely to live near a toxic waste dump than white persons. Fifty percent of Hispanics and 60 percent of blacks live in a community with at least one uncontrollable toxic waste site. Three of the five largest hazardous waste landfills are located in communities that are predominantly black or Hispanic.

- Earth Day is about the destruction of forests, especially tropical forests, and other habitats that is driving 100 species of plants and animals to extinction *every day.* ("For if all the beasts were gone, we might die of a great loneliness.")

- Earth Day is about not splitting off social justice and the destruction of nature from the gross national product. It is about applying the same understanding and sense of relationship to air, soil, and water that the Chipko movement has for trees. "Trees are not wood," they are a living world of plants and animals that offer medicine, food, fuel, and shelter to those who live in and nearby them. They temper climate and refresh air; they hold soil from eroding and assist shallow aquifers in storing water.

- Earth Day is about taking personal action to halt the destruction of our planet, for "the personal is political" and the political can be powerful.

The Earth is not a warehouse, stocked for human use, where we pick and choose what we want and discard the rest. We do not own the Earth, even though many of us own property; companies own forests; and governments lease mineral, water, and fishing rights and control air space. These ways of doing business belie the relationship that we cannot lose sight of, except at our own peril. **The Earth does not belong to us—we belong to the Earth. We humans are a strand in the web.**

❑ ❑ ❑

The land belongs to the future . . . that's the way it seems to me. How many names on the county clerk's plat will be there in fifty years? I might as well try to will the sunset over there to my brother's children. We come and go, but the land is always here. And the people who love it and understand it are the people who own it—for a little while.

Willa Cather, *O Pioneers!* (1913)

About the Author

H. Patricia Hynes is Director of the Institute on Women and Technology and also teaches in the Department of Urban Studies and Planning at the Massachusetts Institute of Technology. An environmental engineer, she served as Section Chief in the Hazardous Waste Division of the U.S. Environmental Protection Agency and Chief of Environmental Management of the Massachusetts Port Authority. For her work in EPA's Superfund program, she won the 1985 Environmental Service Award of the Massachusetts Association of Conservation Commissions. In 1987 she won a German Marshall Fund Environmental Fellowship to do a comparative study of lead contamination and environmental policy in Western Europe and the United States. She is author of *The Recurring Silent Spring* (Pergamon, 1989) and *Reconstructing Babylon; Women and Technology* (Earthscan and Indiana University, 1990).

Long an activist, she founded Bread and Roses, the feminist restaurant and center of culture in Cambridge, Massachusetts in 1974. In 1980 she designed and co-built a passive solar, super-insulated house which served as a model for builders in the Connecticut Valley. Recently she developed an aquifer protection plan for her town of Montague.

227

Index